50 ways to
your Portuguese

Helena Tostevin and
Manuela Cook

Long renowned as the authoritative source for self-guided learning –
with more than 50 million copies sold worldwide – the **Teach Yourself**
series includes over 500 titles in the fields of languages, crafts, hobbies,
business, computing and education.

British Library Cataloguing in Publication Data: a catalogue record
for this title is available from the British Library.

Library of Congress Catalog Card Number: on file.

First published in UK 2010 by Hodder Education, part of Hachette Ul

First published in US 2010 by The McGraw-Hill Companies, Inc.

This edition published 2010.

The **Teach Yourself** name is a registered trade mark of Hachette UK.

Copyright © Helena Tostevin and Manuela Cook 2010

Typeset by MPS Limited, A Macmillan Company.

The publisher has used its best endeavours to ensure that the URLs
for external websites referred to in this book are correct and active
at the time of going to press. However, the publisher and the author
have no responsibility for the websites and can make no guarantee
that a site will remain live or that the content will remain relevant,
decent or appropriate.

Hachette UK's policy is to use papers that are natural, renewable
and recyclable products and made from wood grown in sustainable
forests. The logging and manufacturing processes are expected to
conform to the environmental regulations of the country of origin.

Contents

Choosing the right words

Meet the authors

MANUELA COOK

When I look back at my life, I can see how much of what I do now started in my early childhood. Speaking 'impeccable' Portuguese was a must at home. My sister and I often devised word quizzes for each other. Our parents used to buy us 'serious' books and also cartoons from both Portugal and Brazil, so that we could appreciate the richness and variety of the Portuguese language.

In my adult life, my academic pursuits have been mainly in the area of Linguistics as well as Lusophone Studies, that is, to do with the Portuguese-speaking world. My work in Portuguese language teaching has been a two-way process. I have learned a great deal from my students, at universities and other institutions. Their difficulties and mistakes have given me precious insight into the acquisition of Portuguese as a foreign language. In the light of this I started developing new strategies in the production of learning materials, which I continue to do. I am pleased to be able to share with you the fruits of my experience.

HELENA TOSTEVIN

I have been teaching Portuguese as a foreign language for almost 20 years. It was a career path dictated partially by circumstances, but it has turned into a passion. Other jobs have come and gone, but I cannot give up teaching Portuguese and the enthusiasm for communicating my knowledge of my language to students and watching them develop their linguistic skills is as strong as ever.

I have taught at various institutions, and students of all ages and levels: from beginners to fluent speakers. I have learnt much from them and my contribution to this book is based on their feedback and on the observation of the problems they most frequently encounter.

50 ways to improve your Portuguese is my first foray into book writing. I have been extremely fortunate to be expertly and patiently guided all the way by my very experienced co-author.

Credits

Only got a minute?

Now see what happened …

It was a public place, at the rush hour. A man was trying to open a door. Behind him, a crowd was gathering, hoping to get through.

From the crowd, voices were telling him what to do. 'Push!', he heard. He pushed as hard as he could, but to no avail. Then a lady stepped out to help. She pulled the door open.

She pulled the door open! He couldn't believe it. Weren't they all shouting 'Push!'? The lady explained. What he had heard as 'push' was actually **puxe**, the Portuguese word for *pull*.

The lady and the foreign visitor then had a good chat. She was a teacher of Portuguese Foreign Language and told him she knew straight away he couldn't be a native speaker of Portuguese, when she saw he was pushing instead of pulling. She went on telling him about other words that trip learners up.

There are some features of the Portuguese language that tend to be tricky for English-speaking learners simply because they are different from what you are used to. For instance, in Portuguese words for *my*, *our*, etc. are not used as much as in English. When you would say *'I'm going to drink my coffee'*, in Portuguese you won't need to say the word for *my*, but just **o café**. If you were going to drink someone else's coffee (!), then you would be expected to say whose it was.

The foreign visitor was intending to learn Portuguese, once back home. He would need a course book but he thought it would be handy to also have a book about common pitfalls that would help him start on the right foot. So the next thing he did was to buy *50 ways to improve your Portuguese*.

Only got five minutes?

Then meet Jack and Gill. They wanted to practise the Portuguese they have learned so far, but didn't pay much attention to detail in the classes they attended and overlooked some features of the language which are different from English. As a result communication was not always successful and resulted in several misunderstandings.

First of all, on arrival in a Portuguese-speaking country, they decided that they wanted something to drink and made for the airport café. The waiter did not immediately understand that Gill wanted a cup of tea as she had pronounced the 'ch' of chá the English way instead of the Portuguese way. More embarrassment was to come as Gill then asked for milk, saying, as she would in English, *I'll have some milk*. Again the waiter was slightly confused and wondered initially if she was lactating, but since she didn't have a baby with her, this wasn't the case and it soon dawned on him that she wanted milk for her tea. The waiter was further challenged by Jack's request for a cup of coffee when he said, *May I have some coffee?* Have! Own? Is he asking whether he can buy our café? No, all he wants is a cup of coffee!

Jack and Gill's blunders didn't end when they left the café. In fact the first 24 hours of their visit to this Portuguese-speaking country were blighted by misunderstandings and embarrassments despite their good intentions. They could not figure out how to use the ticket dispensing machine in the metro station and found that they couldn't push the button marked **puxe**. In fact, it wasn't a push-button, but something which needed to be *pulled* and someone in the queue behind them kindly pulled the device out for them.

Their attempts at making small talk with their fellow passengers on the metro train also foundered when Gill attempted to say *We can speak Portuguese*. She remembered **falar Português** but was not aware that a literal translation of *can* would suggest that they were asking for permission to speak the language.

At breakfast in the hotel the next day Jack was asked if he would like a glass of orange juice, but when he heard the word **copo** he thought he was being offered the juice in a cup. Then it was Gill's turn to put her foot in it. She asked for **marmelada**, hoping to get marmalade, but was brought quince paste. What she should have asked for was **geleia de laranja**.

After breakfast they went out, but there were further embarrassments in store. At a supermarket Jack asked for two buns but he forgot to pronounce the 'oi' in **dois** like 'o' in 'note' followed by 'y' in 'yes'. The assistant thought he had said **doze** and began to fill a large bag with twelve buns.

When they arrived at the park with their picnic, they met a couple who were about their age and started making small talk. Gill explained that she was from England and that Jack was from the US. Her actual words were, *I have got an American husband*, forgetting that **um** for *an* was not the best choice in this case and the other couple thought that he was one of many husbands and wanted to know more about her private life. She then went on to explain whereabouts in England she came from, but she used the wrong word for *is* implying that her home town didn't have a fixed location. The word she should have used was é from the verb **ser**.

Thus the conversation didn't go as well as they hoped, and worse still their efforts to be friendly added insult to injury. Despite implications of polygamy and movable municipalities, Jack explained that they were just **pessoas ordinárias** *ordinary people*. He should have said **pessoas comuns**, but mistakenly believed that this meant *common*. He had absolutely no idea that **pessoas ordinárias** meant *vulgar people*. In the same vein, Gill attempted to make a compliment to the woman about her dress. She meant to say *exquisite* but was completely oblivious of the fact that esquisito meant *strange* or *weird*. A more appropriate word would have been **bonito** meaning *pretty, nice, good taste*.

The couple then retreated to a bookshop to see if they could find something that would get their language problems sorted. When the assistant asked them what they were looking for, they could not remember what to use for *for*. They in fact asked for books written by learners of Portuguese. They should have asked for **livros para alunos de português**.

Some good, however, did come out of all these blunders. The shop assistant knew exactly what they needed and the couple now have a book which will put them on the right track, namely *50 ways to improve your Portuguese*.

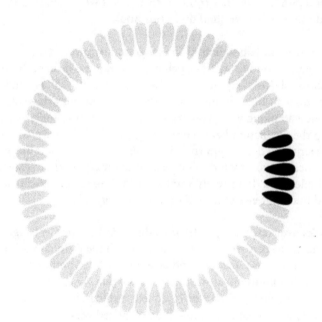

10 Only got ten minutes?

Then take a bird's eye view at blunder prone areas for learners of Portuguese as a foreign language, particularly for those with English as their native or main usage language. Knowing how to spot a pitfall is the best route to ensure you won't fall into it. And that is what we shall do in this book.

To start with, you will need to pay good attention to the Portuguese sounds and the spellings that represent them. If you wish to ask for a cup of tea – **chá** – and utter the 'ch' as you would have done in English, instead of 'sh', the waiter may have difficulty in understanding what you are saying. For nasal sounds, you must keep the distinction between the 'm' as in English 'map' and its different function in **sim** for when you mean to say *yes*. But if what you mean is *no!*, then don't overlook the wavy mark, the so-called **til – não!** You don't really want your 'no!' to sound like 'now!' Find out what else you need to look out for.

Marks over or on a letter (that is, diacritics) are not to be ignored. An acute accent over a vowel can make all the difference. Take for instance **esta**, *this one*, and **está**, *(it) is*. A circumflex accent is equally important. It will differentiate **por**, *by*, from **pôr**, *to put*. The little tail on the 'c', called 'cedilha', is not to be underestimated either. You will be surprised what you may be saying, or writing, if you leave it out – **louça** means *crockery*, **louca** means *mad, insane*.

Ironically, Portuguese words with an English similar counterpart can be tricky to articulate in an intelligible manner. For success, remember to identify which is the right syllable to lay emphasis on. This way people will know you are looking for a **restaurante**, *restaurant*, or that you would like to have your **passaporte**, *passport*, back.

You will also do well in rehearsing some numbers so there isn't an embarrassing confusion. This is the case with **dois** (2), **dez** (10) and **doze** (12). Imagine you are buying train or flight tickets just for yourself and your friend. You mean to ask for two, but what you say sounds like ten or twelve. You'll end up with enough tickets for a whole party!

A different set of sounds, orthographic system and stress pattern can easily trip learners up. Not only will you need to pronounce your Portuguese correctly, but you will also need to decode and use spelling correctly. There is plenty to watch out for in this area.

And this is just the tip of the iceberg. There is more, much more ...

English-speaking learners of Portuguese may need to pay particular attention to some grammatical features that do not have an English equivalent. Two major problem areas are nouns (naming words, like *man* or *cupboard*) and verbs (words for an action or state of being, like *to walk* or *to be*).

It may be pretty obvious that **menino** (*little boy*) and **homem** (*man*) are masculine nouns while **menina** (*little girl*) and **mulher** (*woman*) are feminine; or that **gato** (*male cat*) is masculine but **gata** (*female cat*) is feminine. So far so good! But problems tend to arise with something inanimate, which will also be either masculine or feminine. For grammatical correctness, you will need to know that **armário** (*cupboard*) is masculine but **cadeira** (*chair*) is feminine. You need to find out what to do.

Further to this, you must not lose track of a number of other words that have to 'agree', or match, with the noun, both in gender – masculine or feminine – and number – singular or plural (whether it is one or more). Now things can get really risky! Take for example <u>o</u> armári<u>o</u> nov<u>o</u>, (*the new cupboard*), <u>a</u> porta fechad<u>a</u>, (*the closed door*), **estas cadeiras** (*these chairs*). Again, you need to find out how to achieve this.

English-speaking students often stumble on some features of Portuguese verbs. There is a tendency to overdo the subject pronoun, but, on the other hand, you will need to make sure you can afford to omit it. When and why will it be better to use or leave out the word for *I*, **eu**, in **eu caminho** (*I walk*)? You mustn't forget the required endings – why do you need some additions to **você caminha** (*you walk*) when more than one person are meant? Last, but not least, you mustn't forget to use the right tense and mood (verb form for time and other aspects). When and why will you need to say **quando eu caminhar** (*when I walk*) instead of **quando eu caminho** (*when I walk*)?

In other words, three hazardous zones in verb inflection are the omission, or not, of the personal pronoun subject; some personal endings; and the correct tense and mood. Here again, the absence of a direct equivalent in the English grammatical system is the main cause behind the difficulties experienced.

Problems can also arise in several other areas. Please bear in mind that the Portuguese word for *a/an* – **um**, masculine, and **uma**, feminine – is equally used for number *one*. Consequently, if you mean to talk about your partner, husband or wife, you may wish to avoid the English popular construction *I have a ...* A literal translation of *I have a Brazilian wife* would suggest you have other wives in addition to that one.

There are other popular English renderings that do not translate well into Portuguese. The outcome may range from a slightly confusing to a totally nonsensical statement or question.

The English language uses the possessives (*my, your, his, her,* etc.) much more than Portuguese. A literal translation of *I am going to drink my coffee* – ... **o meu café** – may suggest you had contemplated drinking someone else's.

The English language also uses the verb *to have* much more than Portuguese. A literal translation of *I will have a coffee* – **ter um café** – may suggest something to do with being a café owner.

If you put together these two English favourites – possessives and the verb *to have* – then you may end up with a rather hilarious and absurd statement. A Portuguese literal translation of *I will have my milk* – **ter o meu leite** – said by a woman, may be interpreted as her announcing she is secreting milk, said by a man, it is even more ridiculous!

English-speaking students normally have difficulty with some Portuguese verbs due to a displaced semantic coverage between them and an English verb that covers part of the same meaning but not all. Talking about someone being **alegre** (*happy* or *cheerful*), it may not be easy to discern the difference between **ela é alegre** – verb **ser** (*to be*) – and **ela está alegre** – verb **estar** (*to be*). English *can* will need to be encoded into Portuguese **poder** or **saber**, depending on what is meant. Learners do not always make the right choice when they mean to refer to one's ability to speak Portuguese – **falar Português**. And there are further cases where mistakes are frequent.

Prepositions can be rather slippery. Most learners find it hard to distinguish between **para** and **por** – **Tem um quarto <u>para</u> duas pessoas?**, *Have you got a room <u>for</u> two people?*, **Quanto custa <u>por</u> noite?**, *How much does it cost <u>for</u> a night?* Would you have known which to use?

A preposition contracted with another word can be a recipe for disaster. A dictionary may tell you what you are looking at – **pelo** means *a hair* – while in fact it means *by the* because it is a contraction of two words – **por + o**.

Then there are some sociolinguistic challenges. With their universal *you* as a general form of address, English-speaking students will have to become acquainted with the subtleties between Portuguese **o senhor / a senhora**, **você** and **tu**. Do you have a clear idea of which to opt for, where and when?

Another sociolinguistic challenge is the appropriate use of an expression for *please*, **por favor** or an equivalent polite phrase, to accompany requests. Is this as critical as in English so as to avoid too harsh an approach? To what extent may there already be an element of politeness inbuilt in the Portuguese verb forms used to make a request?

Finally don't fall victim to apparent cross-language synonyms. These 'false friends' can be quite treacherous. They may lead to amusing misunderstandings or have more serious consequences. In practical matters, be aware that what may sound to you like *push*, **puxe**, means *pull*; it may spare you a lot of trouble. When it comes to having a drink, don't forget that **copo** and *cup* are not the same thing. For the fruit preserve you put on your toast at breakfast time, don't get mixed up between **marmelada** and **geleia de laranja**. When socializing and mentioning someone's parents, don't put your foot in it by using the term **parentes.** When trying to make friends, stay clear of howlers by knowing how **esquisito, ordinário,** and **comum** compare with *exquisite, ordinary* and *vulgar*; and learn how **bonito** can rescue you from a sticky situation.

Various factors are responsible for the 50 high incidence 'challenges' unmasked in this book. There are two decisive ones. First, adult learners of a foreign idiom keep falling back into their established linguistic habits, be it pronunciation, grammatical patterns or semantic content. Secondly, unfamiliar traits in the foreign idiom take time to sink in.

Some Portuguese grammatical features which may be alien to an English-speaking learner are associated with the fact that Portuguese is a language of the 'Romance' family. These include gender and number agreement as well as a rich verb inflection, two error prone areas.

The 'Romance' family is a set of languages that descend from vernacular Latin speech, the spoken language of ancient Rome, as it evolved in the different territories of the Roman Empire. Other related languages are, in alphabetical order, Catalan, French, Italian, Romanian, and Spanish.

If you are approaching Portuguese after having learned another of these languages, you can capitalize on their similarities. However, you will need to be careful and remain alert to deceptive appearances. Some similarities may be apparent rather than genuine. If Portuguese is your first 'Romance' language, then you can capitalize on the fact that you will not have any misleading linguistic interference from another idiom in the same group.

We have taken a brief look at error prone areas in the learning of Portuguese, particularly for English-speaking students. We have seen that problems tend to occur in respect of phonetic content, grammatical features and semantic options. If unresolved, these problems will hinder communication and halt the learning process. On the other hand, you will certainly be delighted to find out how easy it is to avoid mistakes once you know what to do.

50 ways to improve your Portuguese has been written to help you overcome these high frequency errors. The book is, accordingly, divided into three main parts, each one focusing on the language from a different angle, namely pronunciation and spelling, structure, and word choice.

This volume is not a replacement for a course book or a grammar manual. It is a complement to them. By anticipating potential weaknesses and finding their remedy, you will be able to progress confidently in your learning of Portuguese knowing that you are bypassing many traps you would otherwise have fallen into.

How to use this book

Learners of a foreign language subconsciously bring into their learning process patterns of linguistic behaviour that are familiar to them, usually from the linguistic environment they grew up in. This often results in mistakes in the new language they are studying.

The purpose of this book is to address these stumbling blocks in the Portuguese language, particularly those that tend to catch out English-speaking learners. Pitfalls are 'isolated' and a solution is given to the problem.

This is not a language course, nor a grammar manual. You will not find an extensive presentation of words and expressions you will need for general communication. Equally, you will not find long lists of rules to follow. What you will find in this book is a selection of frequent mistakes and how to avoid them.

The book consists of three sections, each one looking at several error-prone areas from a distinct angle. In **Sounding right: pronunciation and spelling** the focus is on phonetic features and how they are represented in writing. **Getting the structure right** looks at nouns, verbs and other grammatical categories, as well as at how these words are put together in a sentence. **Choosing the right words** is to do with vocabulary. This last section ends with traps caused by apparent cross-language synonyms, the so-called 'false friends'.

You can use the three sections in two different ways, both as a preventive measure against high incidence mistakes and as a reference guide. Both beginners and more advanced learners should benefit from reading the book systematically, from beginning to end. It is always better to address potential errors before they become entrenched and more difficult to correct. You can also consult a chapter for a specific topic in isolation, even before going through the whole book.

Each time you want to go back to a specific point, you can use the cross-reference **Index,** which takes both a grammar-led and a usage-led approach. This way, if you are unsure about grammatical terms, you can still find what you are looking for. In fact, the whole book is written in simple English and any technical expressions you may come across are explained in the **Glossary of grammatical terms** at the end of the book.

Similarly to what happens between British and American English, there are differences between the Portuguese language on both sides of the Atlantic Ocean, in Portugal and Brazil. Any such relevant differences are shown in the text. What is presented as being specific to Portugal will also apply to countries and other geographical areas in Africa and Asia where Portuguese is spoken. Notwithstanding this, the Portuguese you will find in this book is the standard norm across the Portuguese-speaking world, not regional variants.

An orthographical agreement between the countries where Portuguese is the official language has recently been ratified and is gradually being implemented. It brings some changes to spelling and use of accents. This book has been written within the new specifications. Please be aware that it may take time for the changes to be fully implemented in all the countries involved and you are likely to continue to encounter old spellings for a while.

The choice of the 50 topics you will find in this book is based on our teaching experience. Year in year out, we have seen newcomers to the language stumbling on the same spots. We want you to benefit from our experience and hope the contents of this book will match your needs.

HT and MC

Sounding right: pronunciation and spelling

1 Two by two … and golden silence (**h, ch, nh, lh** – what they stand for)

In Portuguese, letter 'h' has to be handled in quite a different way from English. How to pronounce Portuguese 'h', or not, depends on whether this letter is part of a team or standing on its own.

A Portuguese 'h' on its own is not pronounced. Simply pretend it is not there.

hotel	*hotel*	**h**abitar	*to live in* or *to inhabit*
hospital	*hospital*	**h**ipermercado	*hypermarket*
hospedaria	*inn*	pré-**h**istórico	*prehistoric*
horário	*timetable*	a**h**!	*oh!*
homem	*man*		

In spite of being lazy on its own, as Portuguese 'h' appears to be, it can do a good job when working together with another letter. You will find it in these letter combinations: 'ch', 'nh', and 'lh'.

▶ 'ch' – Watch out! Portuguese 'ch' is not pronounced like the 'ch' in 'cheese' but like 'sh' in 'show'.

chá	*tea*	**ch**eiro	*smell*
chocolate	*chocolate*	**ch**egar	*to arrive*
chave	*key*	a**ch**ar	*to find*
chapéu	*hat*	salsi**ch**a	*sausage*
chuva	*rain*	mo**ch**ila	*rucksack, backpack*
chuveiro	*shower (bathroom)*		

Letter pairs 'nh', and 'lh' – Don't try to separate the 'n' or the 'l' from the 'h'; they go together.

▶ 'nh' – like 'ni' in 'onion'

sen**h**ora	*lady*	un**h**a	*finger/toe nail*
vin**h**o	*wine*	taman**h**o	*size*
ban**h**o	*bath*		

▶ 'lh' – like 'li' in 'million'

mulher	woman	**ilha**	island
filho	son	**colher**	spoon
filha	daughter	**molho**	sauce or gravy
trabalho	work, job		

Insight

Putting this into more grammatical terms, Portuguese 'h' on its own is silent. It does not function as a consonant but rather as a symbol which in most cases shows the word's origin – e.g., <u>h</u>ora (*hour, time*), from Latin **hora**.

However, Portuguese 'h' can be part of a digraph, a group of two letters representing one sound. It is a component in three digraphs – **ch**, **nh** and **lh** – which represent consonantal phonemes (speech sounds). These are all palatal phonemes, made by placing the surface of the tongue against the hard palate, and correspond roughly to the English sounds represented by 'sh', 'ni', and 'li', in respectively *show*, *onion*, and *million*.

2 A hiss, a buzz and a shush (Sounds shown by s and z)

You may find out that letters 's' and 'z' sound as you expect them to when they are at the beginning of a word. In other cases they may play a few tricks on you.

▶ In Portuguese, 's' sounds like 's' in 'so' at the beginning of a word or after a consonant.

sol	sun	**saber**	to know
semana	week	**solteiro**	single, unmarried
senhora	lady	**observar**	to watch
sopa	soup	**sapato**	shoe
sala	room	**seco**	dry
seis	six	**saco**	bag
sete	seven	**absoluto**	absolute
sou	I am		

▶ At the end of a word and often at the end of a syllable, 's' sounds like 'sh' in 'push' in Portugal and in Rio de Janeiro, Brazil, but like 's' in 'so' in most of Brazil.

dois	two	**escada**	stairs
seis	six	**mosca**	fly (insect)
homens	men	**turista**	tourist
esquerda	left	**partidas**	departures
nascer	to be born	**escola**	school
lista	list	**esperar**	to wait
chegadas	arrivals	**mostrar**	to show

▶ Before a voiced consonant, 's' sounds like 's' in 'pleasure' in Portugal and in Rio de Janeiro, Brazil, but like English 'z' in most of Brazil.

mesmo	same	**Lisboa**	Lisbon
desde	since	**desligar**	to disconnect, switch off
desfazer	to undo	**desmanchar**	to undo

4

▶ Between vowels, 's' sounds like English 'z'.

ca_s_a	*house, home*	**blu_s_a**	*blouse*
ca_s_ado	*married*	**bra_s_ileiro**	*Brazilian*
ca_s_al	*couple*	**ga_s_olina**	*petrol*
me_s_a	*table*	**ca_s_aco**	*coat*

▶ In Portuguese, 'z' sounds like English 'z' at the beginning of a word and between vowels.

_z_ero	*zero, nought*	**bu_z_ina**	*car horn*
_z_ebra	*zebra*	**_z_ona**	*area, town*
do_z_e	*a dozen*		*district*
fa_z_er	*to do*		

▶ At the end of a word, 'z' sounds like 'sh' in 'push' in Portugal and Rio de Janeiro, Brazil, but like 's' in 'pleasure' in most of Brazil.

lu_z_	*light*	**nari_z_**	*nose*
feli_z_	*happy*	**pa_z_**	*peace*
carta_z_	*poster*	**de_z_**	*ten*
capu_z_	*hood*	**rapa_z_**	*boy, lad*

▶ Before a voiced consonant, 'z' sounds like 's' in 'pleasure' in Portugal and Rio de Janeiro, Brazil, but like English 'z' in most of Brazil.

Feli_z_ Natal	*Happy Christmas*

Insight

In the flow of speech, 's' and 'z' also sound like English 'z' when they are at the end of a word and the following word starts with a vowel.

Feli_z_ Ano Novo	*Happy New Year*
Feli_z_ Aniversário	*Happy Birthday*
Boa_s_ Entradas	*Happy Start of the New Year/Happy New Year*

3 Let's slide, rock and roll (**s, ss, r, rr**)

You will be seeing double **s** and double **r** in some Portuguese words. You may wonder why and whether just one letter would do. The answer is no.

For 's' to represent sound 's' as in English 'so' when between vowels, we need 'ss'.

pas̲s̲aporte	*passport*	**nos̲s̲o**	*ours*
depres̲s̲a	*quickly*	**as̲s̲inar**	*to sign*

Should you write 'ss' or 's'?

In **cas̲s̲a** the 'ss' sounds like 's' in English 'so', and the word means *muslin (transparent cotton or linen fabric).*

In **cas̲a** the 's' sounds like English 'z'; it means *house* or *home.*

There is a parallel situation with 'r'. You may need to use 'rr' between vowels, depending on what you mean.

Is it 'rr' or 'r'? How different do these words sound?

car̲r̲o	*car*	**car̲o**	*dear or expensive*

A single 'r' between vowels sounds like 'r' in 'bakery'.

car̲o		**bar̲ato**	*cheap, inexpensive*

The 'rr' represents a more forceful sound. It may resemble the rolled Scottish 'r', with a multiple trill, or be closer to 'ch' in 'loch'. It depends on the speaker.

car̲r̲o	*car*	**gar̲r̲afa**	*bottle*
ter̲r̲a	*earth, land*	**sor̲r̲ir**	*to smile*

The sound represented by 'rr' between vowels can also be represented by just one 'r' if at the beginning of a word and generally at the beginning of a syllable.

rua	road, street	**r**ir	to laugh
rio	river	en**r**olar	to roll up
repetir	to repeat	Hen**r**ique	Henry

A single 'r' at the end of a word and generally at the end of a syllable will sound like the 'r' in 'baker' or will be swallowed.

assina**r**	to sign	ma**r**	sea
janta**r**	dinner	ga**r**fo	fork
faze**r**	to do, make	po**r**ta	door
ri**r**	to laugh	ca**r**ne	meat
sorri**r**	to smile		

As you can see, it is important to get these sounds right, 's' or 'ss', 'r' or 'rr'.

ca**s**a or ca**ss**a – do you mean *house* or *muslin*?
ca**r**o or ca**rr**o – do you mean *dear* or *car*?

More embarrassing can be the confusion between verbs **morar**, *to live, to be resident*, and **morrer**, *to die*. The following are the tricky forms:

eu moro, *I live, am resident*, not **eu morro**, *I die*

vocês moraram, *you lived, were resident*, not **vocês morreram**, *you died*

eles/elas moraram, *they (male/female) lived, were resident*, not **eles/elas morreram**, *they died*

Insight
The key lies mainly in rolling or not rolling the 'r'. The verb **morar**, *to live*, has only one 'r'. Don't roll it as you need to do for the 'rr' in **morrer**, *to die*.

4 Play hard or not but mind the tail (Sounds spelt with **qu, g, gu, c** and **ç**)

How to pronounce 'qu' and 'gu' is a recurrent query amongst learners. First, you need to remember that the 'q' sounds like English 'c' in 'cat' and the 'g' like 'g' in 'good'. As for the 'u', a couple of simple rules should help you.

Rule 1

Pronounce 'u' like 'w' in 'water' when the next letter is 'a' or 'o'.

quarto	*room, bedroom*	**gu**arda-chuva	*umbrella*
quanto	*how much*	i**gu**al	*equal, the same*
quando	*when*	á**gu**a	*water*
quota	*quote, share*	lin**gu**agem	*language, speech*

Rule 2

In general, ignore the 'u' when the next letter is either 'e' or 'i'.

quente	*hot*	**gu**erra	*war*
que	*what, that*	**gu**ia	*guide*
queria	*(I) would like*	a**qu**i	*here*
quinze	*fifteen*	se**gu**ir	*to follow*

But there are exceptions for you to learn as you go along where the 'u' is pronounced like 'w' in 'water':

cin**qu**enta	*fifty*	a**gu**entar	*to stand, bear*

We have paired up letter 'q' and letter 'g' for a set of rules that apply to both in the 'qu' and 'gu' sequences. But there is also a fundamental difference between the sounds represented by 'q' and 'g'. Letter 'q' always stands for a hard sound, like 'c' in 'cat'. Letter 'g' can represent a hard sound, as in 'g' in 'good', but also a soft sound, like 's' in pleasure. A comparison with respectively the first and the last 'g' in garage can also be helpful.

Letter 'g' stands for a hard sound before 'u', as we saw above, and before any other letter except e or i.

garrafa	*bottle*	**grande**	*large, big*

In respect of hard and soft options, letter 'g' can be paired up with another letter, 'c', for a set of rules that apply to both.

Rule 1

Both 'c' and 'g' are hard before 'a', 'o' and 'u'.

casa	*house, home*	**curar**	*to treat, cure*
cama	*bed*	**chegar**	*to arrive*
faca	*knife*	**agora**	*now*
copo	*glass, tumbler*	**gostar**	*to like*

Rule 2

Both 'c' and 'g' are soft before 'e' and 'i'.

cem	*a hundred*	**longe**	*far*
cinco	*five*	**bagagem**	*baggage*
gelado	*ice cream*	**viagem**	*journey, voyage*
gente	*people*	**estrangeiro**	*foreign*

Finally, we are going to focus on 'c' and look at a feature peculiar to this letter. We have seen that 'c' is hard before 'a', 'o' and 'u'. Now we are going to see how this can be changed. A mark resembling a little tail can be placed under letter 'c'. This is called 'cedilha' in Portuguese and signals that the 'c' is now soft – 'ç'.

cabeça	*head*	**almoço**	*lunch*
preço	*price*	**açúcar**	*sugar*

5 A DJ and a xylophone in a taxi (Spellings **t**, **d**, **x** and their sounds)

The sounds represented by letters 't', 'd' and 'x' may not be what you expected. Some may vary according to the Portuguese-speaker's country or region. Other causes for variation are mainly related to the word's etymological source, its origin.

Letters 't' and 'd'

In general, letters 't' and 'd' stand for the same speech sound (phoneme), but with one significant difference. Both represent a consonant (a speech sound like 'b', 'c', 'd', etc., where the breath is partially obstructed) where breath obstruction is achieved by raising the front of your tongue inside your mouth. The difference lies in 't' being uttered by breath alone and 'd' being voiced, uttered with the resonance of the vocal cords.

First, we need to see how Portuguese 't' and 'd' compare with their English counterparts, in say, the words 'time' and 'day'. For the Portuguese sounds, raise the tip of your tongue against your front teeth, not gum ridge, so it is less plosive.

Next you need to consider on which side of the Atlantic you will be listening and speaking. In Portugal, the 't' and 'd' sounds are basically the same as in English, but softer, as explained above. For Brazil there is an added feature, a slide of the tongue. A large number of Brazilians pronounce 't' and 'd', particularly before spelling 'e' or 'i' a bit like the 'ch' in 'cheese' and the 'j' in 'jar'. The final '-e' then sounds like 'i' in 'cigarette'. Try saying the following examples in both the Brazilian and the Portuguese way.

quan**t**o	*how much*	**t**ive	*I had*
tu**d**o	*all*	**t**ar**d**e	*afternoon, evening*
dia	*day*	ver**d**a**d**e	*truth*
noi**t**e	*night*	universi**d**a**d**e	*university*

Letter 'x'

In Portuguese, 'x' stands for a number of different sounds. These different sounds have a lot to do with the different origins the respective words have. The good news is that, compared with other letters, 'x' is not much used in portuguese. However, it is present in a few everyday words you are likely to need.

Study the examples in each category below.

▶ Like 'sh' in 'show' at the beginning of a word and in some cases between vowels:

pu<u>x</u>e!	*pull!*	**<u>x</u>arope**	*cough syrup*
<u>x</u>ícara	*cup*	**pei<u>x</u>e**	*fish*
<u>x</u>adrez	*chess*	**li<u>x</u>o**	*rubbish, garbage*

▶ Like 's' in 'so' between two vowels:

pró<u>x</u>imo	*next, near*	**trou<u>x</u>e**	*s/he brought*
má<u>x</u>imo	*maximum*		

▶ Like 'z' in 'zebra' where 'ex' comes before a vowel:

e<u>x</u>ame	*exam*	**e<u>x</u>austo**	*exhausted*
e<u>x</u>emplo	*example*		

▶ Like 'ks' in 'taxi' in some words:

tá<u>x</u>i		**se<u>x</u>o**	*sex*
ane<u>x</u>o	*annexe*	**fi<u>x</u>ar**	*to fix, set*

▶ Like 'sh' for 'show' in Portugal but like 's' for 'so' in most of Brazil before a consonant:

e<u>x</u>tra	*extra*	**se<u>x</u>ta-feira**	*Friday*
e<u>x</u>celente	*excellent*		

6 Surf the sound waves (Nasal sounds)

The Portuguese language is rich in nasal sounds. This is an error-prone area for some learners mainly due both to an unclear notion of how these speech sounds are achieved and to how they are represented in spelling.

In English, nasal sounds are represented by consonants 'm', 'n', and also '-ng', as in '<u>m</u>other', '<u>n</u>o', 'si<u>ng</u>'. These are consonants (speech sounds produced with partial obstruction of the air flow) in which the air stream passes through the nose as a result of the lowering of the soft palate at the back of the mouth while the mouth is occluded at some point by the lips or tongue. The Portuguese nasal phenomenon is not too dissimilar.

'm-' and 'n-'

In Portuguese, letters 'm' and 'n' represent nasal consonants very much like their English counterparts, at the beginning of a word or a syllable, as in the following examples:

<u>m</u>esa	*table*	**<u>n</u>ome**	*name*
<u>n</u>ada	*nothing*	**se<u>m</u>a<u>n</u>a**	*week*

'-m' and '-n'

In Portuguese, letters 'm' and 'n' also appear at the end of a word or a syllable to represent a nasal sound but here they are not functioning as a consonant. In this case the nasal sound is a vowel (a speech sound derived from 'a', 'e', 'i', 'o', 'u' with vibration of the vocal cords and no significant breath obstruction).

Don't try to pronounce '-m' and '-n' as consonants. Simply look at the vowel sound that comes before them and pronounce it letting the air flow find its way out through the nasal tract. Try these:

s<u>im</u>	*yes*	**at<u>um</u>**	*tuna*
<u>um</u>	*one; a/an*	**<u>am</u>bos**	*both*
f<u>im</u>	*end*	**<u>em</u>**	*in, on*
b<u>om</u>	*good*	**baga<u>gem</u>**	*baggage*

banco	bank	conta	bill
centro	centre	mundo	world
cinco	five	ontem	yesterday

The little wave, ~

Another way of showing a nasal vowel sound is by using a wave-like mark over it – irmã (*sister*), maçã (*apple*). This mark is called **til** in Portuguese.

You will often see the **til** over one of a set of two vowels – não. In this case we have a diphthong (where articulation begins as for one vowel and moves as for another, as in English word 'coin') which is nasal. The **til** plays a dual role, both showing this is a nasal diphthong and pointing to the segment that must be pronounced more forcefully. Some examples for you to practise:

não	no	pão	bread	põe	s/he puts
mãe	mother	são	they are	nações	nations
irmão	brother	pães	loaves		

Don't ignore the wavy mark. The **til** is there to remind you of a nasal sound. The same set of sounds may have different meanings depending on whether you just use your mouth or seek a little help from your nose.

a (oral)	mau	bad, evil	a (oral)	pais	fathers(male
ã (nasal)	mão	hand			parents), parents
			ã (nasal)	pães	bread loaves

| a (oral) | mais | more | a (oral) | cais | quay |
| ã (nasal) | mães | mothers | ã (nasal) | cães | dogs |

The best is to go with the **til**… and surf the wave.

....

Insight

'am' (campo, *field, country*), 'em' (sempre, *always*), 'en' (pente, *comb*), 'im' (sim, *yes*) function as a digraph (a group of two letters representing one speech sound). Don't pronounce the 'm' or 'n' as a separate consonant!

....

7 High and low (Upper and lower case letters)

Don't overdo capital letters. In Portuguese they are used more sparingly than in English.

▶ Use an initial capital letter with proper nouns (name of a person or place):

Adriano é de Cabo Verde, um país da África, localizado no Oceano Atlântico.
Adriano is from Cabo Verde, a country in Africa, situated in the Atlantic Ocean.

▶ Do not use an initial capital letter for nationalities, months, days of the week or seasons:

Ela é brasileira e vai chegar no sábado dia 7 de agosto, que é pleno verão em Portugal.
She is Brazilian and is going to arrive on Saturday August 7th, which is mid-summer in Portugal.

▶ Points of the compass:

(a) do not use an initial capital letter for their names, only for their abbreviations:

norte but **N** *North*   **sudeste** but **SE** *Southeast*

(b) but take capitals when part of an established geographical name or defining a region:

Vivo no Norte.
I live in the North. (northern part of the country)

Conheço a América do Norte melhor que a América do Sul.
I know North America better than South America.

▶ Use initial capitals for:

(a) religious and other festivities:

Passamos o Natal com a família.
We spend Christmas with our family.

(b) names of institutions:

A sede do Instituto Camões é em Lisboa.
Instituto Camões has its headquarters in Lisbon.

▶ The use of initial capitals is optional in the following situations:

(a) in names of academic disciplines:

Estudei português. or	*I have studied*
Estudei Português.	*Portuguese.*

(b) in forms of address

Senhor Doutor Galvão or	*Doctor Galvão.*
senhor doutor Galvão	

▶ Use capitals in abbreviations formed by initials:

CPLP – Comunidade dos Países de Língua Portuguesa
Community of Portuguese Language Countries

▶ In titles of works it is normal to capitalize the first word and all the following main words but not short words like articles – o/a, *the*, etc. – prepositions – **de**, *of*, etc. – and conjunctions – e, *and*, etc.

O Cão e os Caluandas, romance do escritor angolano Pepetela
'O Cão e os Caluandas', a novel by Angolan writer Pepetela
A Varanda do Frangipani, do autor moçambicano Mia Couto
'A Varanda do Frangipani', by Mozambican author Mia Couto

You must follow these rules when writing an essay in Portuguese.

8 Beat the drums (Stress and graphic accent)

We are now going to look at the beat of the music. Newcomers to a language tend to cling to the stress pattern of their native tongue. Trying to pronounce Portuguese words the English way won't work. In fact, it is a main source of mispronunciation and miscommunication.

So that you stress the right syllable, or segment, in the word, you need to remember the following: with some exceptions, Portuguese words have a syllable that is pronounced more forcefully than the others. In general, this is the penultimate syllable.

pal<u>a</u>vra – *word*

The pull towards your familiar stress pattern is likely to be stronger in words you can identify with an English equivalent, but now you know better. Try the following:

passap<u>o</u>rte   **restau<u>ran</u>te**   **choco<u>la</u>te**   **universi<u>da</u>de**

Not all Portuguese words are stressed on the next-to-last syllable. In words which do not end in a single 'a', 'e', or 'o', the stress usually falls on the last syllable.

ho<u>tel</u>

Try these words too:

fa<u>vor</u>   **profe<u>ssor</u>**   **jan<u>tar</u>**   **fa<u>zer</u>**
fe<u>liz</u>   **a<u>zul</u>**

For words that do not follow the rule, you can expect a graphic accent to direct you to the right syllable. This mark is placed over a vowel, never a consonant, and can do a double job. It can indicate both a stressed syllable and the quality of its vowel content. These two features are inter-related. We often change the quality of a vowel when we stress the syllable where that vowel is.

<u>á</u>gua

The marked '<u>á</u>' is pronounced more forcefully than the final 'a' (the former resembles English 'a' in 'ah', the latter 'a' as in 'among').

There are three different written accents in Portuguese. The acute accent, a right-to-left oblique mark ('), the grave accent, a left-to-right oblique mark (`), and the circumflex accent, where two oblique lines meet in a hat-like shape (^). For example, in the word **pé** (*foot*) the acute accent shows the 'e' is to be pronounced similarly to English 'e' in 'tell', in the word **vo<u>cê</u>** (*you*) the circumflex accent shows it is to be pronounced differently, more like English 'e' in 'they' (without the final glide). The grave accent on 'à' shows an open sound as a result of two contracted particle words, preposition 'a' (*to, at*) and definite article 'a' (*the*). Signalling the stressed syllable is the other role played by the accents – vo<u>cê</u>, **<u>pró</u>ximo** (*next, near*).

Here are some more words for you to try:

<u>á</u>rea	*area*	**<u>trân</u>sito**	*traffic*
pal<u>á</u>cio	*palace*	**<u>lâm</u>pada**	*light bulb*
<u>fá</u>cil	*easy*	**<u>pês</u>sego**	*peach*
a<u>çú</u>car	*sugar*	**portu<u>guês</u>**	*Portuguese*

9 Make a difference (Accurate spelling)

As a matter of good practice, you should always learn a new word with its accent, where there is one. If you omit an accent when you are writing, your message could probably still be understood. However, there may be problems if the accent signals a different meaning of the word and the context isn't clear.

So, beware of these (by no means an exhaustive list):

e	*and*	**é**	*(it) is* (from **ser**)
a	*the* (*) or *to/at*	**à**	*to/at the* (*)
esta	*this* (*)	**está**	*(it) is* (from **estar**)
se	*if*	**Sé**	*See (cathedral)*
pais	*parents*	**país**	*country*
por	*by, through*	**pôr**	*to put*
da	*of the* (*)	**dá**	*(he/she) gives*
avô	*grandfather*	**avó**	*grandmother*
inicio	*(I) start*	**início**	*(the) beginning*
fabrica	*(he/she) manufactures*	**fábrica**	*factory*
habito	*(I) live*	**hábito**	*habit*
medica/o	*(he/she) medicates/ (I) medicate*	**médica/o**	*doctor (female/male)*

(*)the feminine singular form

You'll have noticed that the last four examples are of a similar nature: the word without accent is a form of the verb (doing or being word), the other the corresponding noun (naming word). There are many more instances like these.

Within the verb category, an accent can be an indicator of person (who does/did/will do what) and other relevant aspects, mainly tense (when the action takes/took/will take place). We are going to look at some examples of how this is achieved.

Who does, did or will do what and when

▶ t**e͟**m, t**ê͟**m – verb **ter** (*to have*)

In Portuguese the personal subject pronoun (*I, you, s/he,* etc.) is often omitted when information on who does/did/will do something is built into the verb form. In **tem** we know it is singular (one person), and in **têm** plural (more than one). There may be no need to use the pronoun, thanks to the accent (^).

| (ele) **T͟em um carro novo.** | *He has a new car.* |
| (eles) **T͟êm um carro novo.** | *They have a new car.* |

Similarly,

▶ v**e͟**m, v**ê͟**m – verb **vir** (*to come*)

In **vem** we know one person is meant, and in **vêm** more than one.

| (ele) **V͟em para Lisboa.** | *He is coming to Lisbon.* |
| (eles) **V͟êm para Lisboa.** | *They are coming to Lisbon.* |

▶ p**o͟**de, p**ô͟**de – verb **poder** (*can, to be able to*)

The two forms **pode – pôde** denote different tenses. In this case we may be able to omit an expression of time, for instance **passado** and **que vem**.

| **Ele pô͟de visitar o castelo no domingo (passado).** | *He was͟ able to visit the castle last͟ Sunday.* |
| **Ele po͟de visitar o castelo no domingo (que vem).** | *He is going to be͟ able to visit the castle this coming͟ Sunday.* |

Insight

The correct use of an accent extends beyond orthographic accuracy. It conveys a message and it is important to get it right!

10 Tune yourself to success (Subtle sounds)

There are some subtle sound distinctions that tend to catch unawares anyone learning Portuguese as a foreign language:

o and e sounds

When stressed, the quality of the vowels 'o' and 'e' may change. We see this:

▶ in some nouns, when they change from singular to plural:

ovo – ovos   *egg – eggs*
porto – portos   *port, harbour – ports, harbours*

In these examples, in the singular the closed 'o' in the stressed syllable is pronounced like 'o' in 'note' but in the plural it is an open 'o' pronounced like 'o' in 'jolly'.

▶ in a number of cases, according to the vowel in the following syllable:

(o) bolo – (a) bola

In **bolo**, *cake*, the first o is like 'o' in *note*; in **bola**, *ball*, the first o is like 'o' in 'jolly'.

como – come

In **como** (*how, as* or verb form *I eat*) the first o is like 'o' in 'note'; in **come** (verb form, *you eat*) the first o *is* like 'o' in 'jolly'.

(o) olho – olha!

In the noun **olho**, *eye*, the first o is like 'o' in 'note'; in the verb form **olha** (*look*), the first o is like 'o' in jolly.

▶ in the words for *he* and *she* and others that follow the same pattern. In masculine forms, the first 'e' is pronounced like 'e' in 'they' but without the final glide. In feminine forms the first 'e' is pronounced like 'e' in 'tell':

e̲le / e̲la	*he/she*
e̲ste / e̲sta	*this, this one* (masculine/feminine)
e̲sse / e̲ssa	*that, that one* (masculine/feminine)
aque̲le / aque̲la	*that, that one* (masculine/feminine)

Difficult sounds in numbers

Some numbers may sound similar and cause confusion like '-ty' and '-teen' in English. Have a good look at the following sets of numbers which are easily confused:

▶ **dois** (2), **dez** (10) or **doze** (12)

Listen carefully for the sounds shown by 'oi', 'e' and 'o':

'oi': like 'o' in 'note' + 'y' in 'yet'
'e': like 'e' in 'tell'
'o': like 'o' in 'note'

▶ **três** (3) or **treze** (13)

Listen carefully for the sounds shown by 's' and 'z':

's': like 'sh' in 'push' (in Portugal) or like 's' in 'us' (in Brazil)
'z': like 'z' in 'zebra'

▶ **sessenta** (60) or **setenta** (70)

Listen out for the sounds shown by 'ss' and the first 't':

'ss': like 's' in 'so'
't': like English 't' but softer

Getting the structure right

11a Eu viajo frequentemente entre o Brasil e Portugal
I travel frequently between Brazil and Portugal
(The definite article)

In English, the definite article is *the*, but in Portuguese it changes according to whether the noun it is related to is masculine or feminine, singular or plural.

o	masculine singular	**o homem**	*the man*
a	feminine singular	**a mulher**	*the woman*
os	masculine plural	**os meninos**	*the little boys*
as	feminine plural	**as meninas**	*the little girls*

For English-speaking learners pitfalls arise from the fact that the Portuguese definite article is much more widely used than its English counterpart.

Look carefully at the following examples where the article is used.

▶ continents:

A África é maior que a Europa. *Africa is larger than Europe.*
A Europa é um continente *Europe is a relatively small*
relativamente pequeno. *continent.*

▶ many countries (though not Portugal and some other Portuguese-speaking countries – Angola, Cabo Verde, Moçambique, São Tomé e Príncipe, Timor – and Cuba, Israel, Marrocos and a few others):

O Brasil é o país mais vasto da *Brazil is the largest country*
América do Sul. *in South America.*

In some cases, however, it may or may not be used.

A Inglaterra faz parte do Reino *England is part of the United*
Unido. *Kingdom.*
Ele vai para (a) Inglaterra. *He is going to England.*

▶ generally, with place names where the name also has a general meaning:

O Porto fica no norte de Portugal.   *Porto is in northern Portugal.*
(**porto** as a common noun means *port, harbour*.)
A Guarda é uma cidade portuguesa.   *Guarda is a Portuguese town.*
(**guarda** as a common name means *guard*.)
Os Açores são ilhas do Oceano   *The Azores are islands in the*
  Atlântico.   *Atlantic Ocean.*
(**açor** as a common name means *goshawk*)

▶ often with the names of languages:

O Português é falado em várias   *Portuguese is spoken in*
  partes do mundo.   *several parts of the world.*

▶ with nouns used in a general sense:

A água não deve ser desperdiçada.   *Water should not be wasted.*

▶ with the names of meals:

Por favor, fique para o jantar.   *Please stay for dinner.*

▶ with the names of seasons:

O verão é a minha estação favorita.   *Summer is my favourite*
     season.

▶ with the names of religious and other festivals:

Este ano a Páscoa é cedo.   *This year Easter is early.*
Vou passar o Natal em casa.   *I'm going to spend Christmas*
     at home.

▶ with the days of the week:

Para mim o domingo é o   *For me Sunday is the best day*
  melhor dia da semana.   *of the week.*

11b Eu vou passar as férias com a minha amiga
I am going to spend my holidays with my friend
(The definite article continued)

Further to the examples shown in 11a, in Portuguese the definite article is also used in a number of other situations:

▶ with names of people, particularly in the spoken language and referring to someone you know (mainly in Portugal):

A Rita mora perto. *Rita lives nearby.*

▶ when referring to someone with a title:

Este é o Doutor Carlos Machado. *This is Doctor Carlos Machado.* (introducing Carlos Machado)

▶ with the possessive adjectives and pronouns:

Esta é a minha amiga. *This is my friend.*
Esta mala é a minha. *This suitcase is mine.*

▶ with parts of the body (where English would have used a possessive):

Vou cortar o cabelo. *I am going to have my hair cut.*

▶ with clothing and belongings (where English uses a possessive):

Não esqueça o guarda-chuva. *Don't forget your umbrella.*

▶ with nouns relating to the self (where English uses a possessive):

Eu vou passar as férias na praia. *I am going to spend my holidays at the seaside.*

Please also note that the definite article:

▶ is used with the word **casa** in the sense of *house* but not in the sense of *home*.

Esta é a casa da Laura.	*This is Laura's house.*
Agora vou para casa.	*Now I am going home.*

▶ is often repeated when listing more than one person or item.

O diretor e o gerente da empresa estavam presentes na reunião.	*The company's director and manager were present at the meeting.*

(Saying o **diretor e gerente** ... would suggest one individual playing both roles.)

▶ tends to be repeated with the second term of an opposite.

a vida e a morte	*life and death*

The 'definite article' that is not a definite article

O carro da Ana e o da Teresa	*Ana and Teresa's car* (**o** = the one that belongs to Teresa)
As malas do Roberto e as do Jorge	*Roberto and Jorge's suitcases* (**as** = those that belong to Jorge)

Both o and **as** in these two examples are pronouns (words that stand for a noun) standing for respectively **carro** and **malas**.

....

Insight

Don't confuse the Portuguese definite article **a** with the indefinite article (*a/an*) – **a mala** is not *a suitcase* but *the suitcase*.

a mala e o casaco	*the suitcase and the coat*
as malas e os casacos	*the suitcase and the coats*
a mala e as luvas	*the suitcase and the gloves*

....

12 Cem carros em meia hora, que boa ideia!
A hundred cars in half an hour, what a good idea!
(The indefinite article)

The indefinite article is *a/an* in English, but in Portuguese is **um, uma, uns, umas** depending on the gender and number of the noun it governs.

um	masculine singular	**um homem**	*a man*
uma	feminine singular	**uma mulher**	*a woman*
uns	masculine plural	**uns meninos**	*some little boys*
umas	feminine plural	**umas meninas**	*some little girls*

English-speaking learners often confuse Portuguese **a** with the indefinite article. You need to remember that the Portuguese article **a** is the definite article and translates *the* – **a** menina, *the little girl*.

You also need to be aware of the situations where English uses *a/an* (but Portuguese does not). See below:

▶ with nouns expressing profession or occupation, affiliation, marital status or origin:

Ele é advogado.	*He is a lawyer.*
Ele é católico.	*He is a Catholic.*
Ele é viúvo.	*He is a widower.*

▶ when expressing the stages of life:

Ele já é adulto.	*He is an adult* (literally, *he is already adult*).
Ela ainda é criança.	*She is a child* (literally, *she is still child*).

▶ when expressing hundreds and thousands:

cem carros	*a hundred cars*
mil palavras	*a thousand words*

▶ when expressing *half a*:

meia hora	*half an hour*

- when expressing *What a ...!*
  Que boa ideia!   *What a good idea!*

- with phrases giving more information about a noun:
  O Algarve, zona turística,   *The Algarve, a tourist area, is in*
  fica no sul de Portugal.   *Southern Portugal.*

Some of these differences are associated with the fact that Portuguese **um** and **uma** also function as a numeral, meaning *one*. The notion of number is never too far away in one's mind. If you mean to say *I have a foreign husband* and translate it literally as **Tenho um marido estrangeiro** (**um** = *a*, but also **um** = *one*), you may be inviting a comment along the lines of *How many husbands have you got then?* A Portuguese native speaker would more likely say **(O) meu marido é estrangeiro**, *My husband is foreign.*

By the same token, the notion of number also creeps in with plural forms **uns e umas.**

Eu vou comprar maçãs.	*I am going to buy apples.*
Eu vou comprar umas maçãs.	*I am going to buy some (= a few) apples.*

13 Li o jornal durante a viagem *I read the paper on the journey* (Gender and nouns)

Portuguese nouns are either masculine or feminine. This applies to human beings and animals – so far so good – but also to inanimate things. You may wonder how you are going to remember if a chair is masculine or feminine.

The safest way to avoid mistakes is to always learn a word with its definite article, the **o** (masculine) or **a** (feminine) before it.

There are also some general rules that help.

▶ A noun ending in **o** is likely to be masculine and one in **a** feminine:

o menino	*little boy*	**a menina**	little girl
o indivíduo	*individual, person*	**a pessoa**	person
o adulto	*adult*	**a criança**	child
o carro	*car*	**a casa**	house
o armário	*cupboard*	**a cadeira**	chair
o banco	*bank*	**a saída**	exit
o câmbio	*foreign exchange*	**a alfândega**	customs
um adulto	*an adult*	**uma criança**	a child
um banco	*a bank*	**uma saída**	an exit, a way out

But some everyday exceptions include **o** / **um dia**, *day* and **o** / **um mapa**, *map*.

▶ You can expect a noun to be feminine if it ends in:

'-gem'

a viagem	*journey*	**a bagagem**	*baggage*
a garagem	*garage*		

'-dade'

a cidade	*town, city*	**a universidade**	*university*
a verdade	*truth*		

'-tude'

a juventude	*youth*	**a solicitude**	*thoughtfulness*

'-ão' (when the English translation of the word ends in -tion):

a estação	*station*	**a informação**	*information*
a tradição	*tradition*		

▶ Nouns ending in 'l' or 'r' are often masculine:

o jornal	*newspaper*	**o computador**	*computer*
o hotel	*hotel*	**o hospital**	*hospital*
o futebol	*soccer*	**o lugar**	*place*

But look out for nouns which are both masculine and feminine according to their meaning:

A capital de Portugal é Lisboa.	*The capital of Portugal is Lisbon.*
O capital da empresa aumentou.	*The capital of the company has increased.*
Tenho um guia de S. Paulo muito completo.	*I have a very comprehensive guidebook of S. Paulo.*
A nossa guia é muito sabedora.	*Our guide (female) is very knowledgeable.*

··

Insight

You need to remember that the words **a pessoa** (*person*), o adulto (*adult*) and **a criança** (child) are used when referring to both males and females.

dois adultos, um homem e uma mulher (os adultos)	*two adults, a man and a woman*
duas crianças, um menino e uma menina (as crianças)	*two children, a boy and a girl*
cinco pessoas, dois homens, duas mulheres e uma criança (as pessoas)	*five people, two men, two women and a child*

··

14 O que é isto? Um chapéu vermelho! *What is this? A red hat!* (Gender and different words)

The grammatical gender of nouns extends to other words that come under different grammatical categories. Mistakes often occur when you forget this.

Try to remember the following examples.

▶ Adjectives – words like *red* and *good*:

Masculine	Feminine	
fri**o**	fri**a**	*cold*
vermelh**o**	vermelh**a**	*red*
bonit**o**	bonit**a**	*pretty*
b**o**m	bo**a**	*good*
est**e**	est**a**	*this*

a águ**a** fri**a**	*cold water*
o carr**o** vermelh**o**	*the red car*
um chapéu bonit**o**	*a pretty hat*
Est**e** quart**o** é b**o**m.	*This bedroom is good.*

▶ Past participles – words like *open* or *closed*:

Masculine	Feminine	
fechad**o**	fechad**a**	*closed*
abert**o**	abert**a**	*open*
proibid**o**	proibid**a**	*prohibited*
obrigad**o**	obrigad**a**	*thank you* (more literally, *grateful*)

A loj**a** está fechad**a**.	*The shop is closed.*
O restaurante está abert**o**.	*The restaurant is open.*
Estacionament**o** proibid**o**	*No parking (parking prohibited)*

Entrada proibida	*No entry (entry prohibited)*
Obrigado (said by male)	*Thank you*
Obrigada (said by female)	*Thank you*

▶ Ordinal numbers – words like *first, second,* etc.:

Masculine	Feminine	
primeiro	**primeira**	*first*
segundo	**segunda**	*second*

terceiro andar	*third floor –* (**o**) *andar*
décima quarta lição	*fourteenth lesson –* (**a**) *lição*

▶ Pronouns – words like *this one*:

Masculine	Feminine	
este	**esta**	*this one*
aquele	**aquela**	*that one*

Quero este.	*I want this one.* (referring for example to **o pão,** *loaf of bread*)
Quero aquela.	*I want that one.* (referring for example to **a garrafa,** *bottle*)

15 Aquela estudante europeia tem uma irmã dentista
That European female student has a sister who is a dentist (Changing masculine to feminine)

Although many nouns (naming words) and adjectives (describing or qualifying words) become feminine by changing the final '-o' to '-a', this is not always the case. You will need to remember a few rules so as to avoid errors.

▶ A large number of words ending in '-o' substitute 'a':

amigo → amiga	*friend, male → female*
filho → filha	*son → daughter*
neto → neta	*grandson → granddaughter*
médico → médica	*doctor, male → doctor, female*
enfermeiro → enfermeira	*nurse, male → nurse, female*
brasileiro → brasileira	*Brazilian man → Brazilian woman*

▶ Words ending in '-or' or '-ês' add '-a':

senhor → senhora	*gentleman → lady*
inglês → inglesa (no accent ^ in the feminine)	*English man → woman*
português → portuguesa	*Portuguese man → Portuguese woman*

▶ Words ending in '-eu' in general substitute '-eia':

europeu → europeia	*European, male → female*

▶ Words ending in '-e' or '-a' do not change:

estudante	*student, male → female*
dentista	*dentist, male → female*
motorista	*driver, male → female*

▶ Some words in '-ão' drop the final '-o':

irmão → irmã	*brother → sister*

▶ Some words in '-ão' change to '-ona':

brincalhão → **brincalhona** *playful, male → female*

▶ Some words in '-ão' change to '-oa':

patrão → **patroa** *boss, master, male → female*

▶ A different word is used:

pai → **mãe** *father → mother*

▶ '-ô' changes to '-ó':

avô → **avó** *grandfather → grandmother*

▶ The words for *good* and *bad* are irregular.

bom → **boa**	*good, nice, fine*
mau → **má**	*bad, evil, wicked*

um hotel bom	*a good/nice hotel*
uma praia boa	*a good/nice beach*
um dia bom	*a nice day*
um dia mau	*a wicked day*
Que coisa tão boa!	*What a nice thing (to happen)!*
Que coisa tão má!	*What a wicked thing (to happen)!*

The above examples for **mau-má** reflect Brazilian practice – Brazilians tend to be euphemistic about something that is bad (**não é bom**) and use **mau-má** if they mean wicked or evil.

Insight

Please remember these changes:

-or → -ora	**-ão → -ã**
-ês → -esa	**-ão → -ona**
-eu → -eia	**-ô → -ó**

16 Eles compraram dez pães e dois guarda-chuvas azuis *They bought ten bread loaves and two blue umbrellas* (Plurals)

Most Portuguese nouns, like English ones (and adjectives, unlike English), end in an '-s' when there is more than one (e.g., 1 **carro** → 2 **carros** (*cars*). However, there are some nouns and adjectives which don't follow this pattern and you will need to look carefully at the following examples to avoid making mistakes.

▶ Words ending in a consonant other than '-m' or '-l' add '-es':

mulher → **mulheres** *women*

but words ending in '-ês' lose the accent in the plural:

português → **portugueses** *Portuguese*

▶ Words ending in '-m' substitute '-ns':

homem → **homens** *men*

▶ Words ending in '-al' substitute '-ais':

hospital → **hospitais** *hospitals*

Sometimes the plural ending depends on whether the singular ending is stressed or not. In these cases we have marked the singular ending (+) for stressed or (-) for unstressed.

▶ Words ending in '-el' (-) substitute '-eis'; those ending in '-el' (+) substitute '-éis':

automóvel → **automóveis** *automobiles*
hotel → **hotéis** *hotels*

▶ Words ending in '-il' (-) substitute '-eis'; those ending in '-il' (+) substitute '-is':

fácil	→ **fáceis**	*easy*
gentil	→ **gentis**	*courteous*

▶ Words ending in '-ol' (-) substitute '-ois'; those ending in '-ol' (+) substitute '-óis':

álcool	→ **álcoois**	*alcohols*
lençol	→ **lençóis**	*bed sheets*

▶ Words ending in '-ul' substitute '-uis':

azul	→ **azuis**	*hands*

▶ There are three different plural forms for words ending in '-ão'. Some take an '-s', some change to '-ões', and others to '-ães':

mão	→ **mãos**	*hands*
avião	→ **aviões**	*aeroplanes*
pão	→ **pães**	*bread loaves*

▶ Some words have only one form for both singular and plural:

lápis → **lápis** *pencil*   **cais** → **cais** *quay*

▶ Compound words form their plurals in more than one way. In words consisting of noun, adjective, ordinals, etc. + noun, both elements take a plural ending: **quinta-feira** → **quintas-feiras** *Thursdays* (**quinta** meaning *fifth*); **couve-flor** → **couves-flores** (*cauliflowers*) (**couve** (*cabbage*) + **flor** (*flower*)).

In words consisting of verb, etc. + noun, only the noun takes a plural ending: **guarda-chuva** → **guarda-chuvas** (*umbrellas*) (**guarda**, from **guardar**, *to guard, protect*).

Insight

A masculine plural noun may include both genders: **amigos** are male friends but also male and female friends, and **pais** are fathers (male parents) but also parents (father and mother).

17 Bom dia e um dia bom! *Good morning, and a nice day!* (Word order in nouns and adjectives)

In Portuguese, adjectives are usually placed after the noun they are describing or qualifying. They can also be found before the noun. Their position plays a role. Insight on how this works will help you make your choices with confidence.

NOUN + ADJECTIVE

This arrangement is used mainly for factual descriptions:

Ontem eu tive um <u>dia bom</u>.   *Yesterday I had a good day.*

ADJECTIVE + NOUN

This arrangement is used mainly for qualifying (with an element of emphasis):

Bom dia!   *Good morning!*

This is a morning greeting, to wish someone a *Good day!*

In these two sentences, the adjective **bom** has two different shades of meaning. See some more examples.

um <u>livro grande</u>	*a large book*
um <u>grande livro</u>	*a great book*
uma <u>casa velha</u>	*an old house*
um <u>velho amigo</u>	*an old friend*
uma <u>camisa cara</u>	*an expensive shirt*
<u>Cara Rita</u>	*Dear Rita (in letter writing)*

Other words, such as past participles (*closed*, etc.), used adjectively, and ordinals (*first*, etc.) also fall into this word order pattern:

porta fechada	*closed door*
terceira rua	*third road*

Further information on a noun can be provided by a second noun in both English and Portuguese, but the way the words are put together can be quite different.

The sequence

noun + **de** + noun

is often used in Portuguese:

a **bagagem de mão**	*hand baggage* (literally, *baggage of hand*)
o **fim de semana**	*weekend* (literally, *end of week*)
uma **bagagem de mão pesada**	*a heavy item of hand baggage*
um **bom fim de semana para você**	*a good weekend to you (I wish you a good weekend)*

18a A casa nova é bonita *The new house looks nice* (Gender and number agreement)

Adjectives agree in gender (masculine or feminine) and number (singular or plural) with the noun they describe or qualify, which may be an unfamiliar concept to you and, as such, an area of uncertainty. You just need to know what it's all about and you will find out it is quite easy to master.

GENDER

a camisa branca   *the white shirt*

The word **camisa** (a noun) is feminine. This is shown by its ending in '-a' and the preceding article **a**. The word for *white* (an adjective) also takes the ending '-a'. So both s*hirt* and *white* go hand in hand showing they are of the same kind. This is what is meant by agreement.

o chapéu preto   *the black hat*

The noun **chapéu** is masculine. This may not be obvious from its ending, but gender information is provided by the preceding article **o**. The adjective, *black*, also takes an '-o', so both noun and adjective agree.

NUMBER

os sapatos verdes   *green shoes*

'-o' tells us that **sapato** is masculine, but the '-s' throughout indicates that more than one shoe is meant and they are green.

With nouns consisting of more than one element, the adjective agrees in gender and number with its leading component.

os guarda-chuvas amarelos   *the yellow umbrellas*
os fins de semana agradáveis   *the pleasant weekends I spent*
 que eu passei

ADJECTIVES AND PRONOUNS

Adjectives also agree in gender and number with a pronoun (a word standing in for a noun) they describe or qualify.

Este é bom.	*This one is good.* (you are referring to **o chapéu,** for example)
Aquela é boa.	*That one is good.* (you are referring to **a camisa,** for example)
Isto é bom.	*That one is good.* (this thing, a masculine ending with a neuter function)

AGREEING WITH ABSENT NOUNS AND PRONOUNS

An adjective can still agree with a noun or pronoun even if they are not present in the phrase or sentence.

Que lind<u>o</u>!   *How beautiful!*

(You are commenting, for example, on something you are looking at.)

O CARRO NOVO É RÁPIDO.

18b As portas estão fechadas e as janelas abertas
The doors are closed and the windows open
(Gender and number agreement)

In 18a we saw that adjectives agree in gender and number with the noun they describe or qualify. Adjective-like words behave in a similar way.

Past participles (*tired*, etc.) used adjectively follow the same agreement pattern as adjectives.

The next three examples show how the past participle of **cansar** (*to tire*) can be used adjectivally – look out for the agreement in number and gender:

Ele está cansado.	*He is tired.*
Ela está cansada.	*She is tired.*
Eles estão cansados.	*They are tired.*

Here are examples using the past participles of **acender** (*to switch on*), **apagar** (*to switch off*), **desligar** (*to disconnect*), **fechar** (*to close*), and **abrir** (*to open*):

A luz está acesa.	*The light is on.* (literally *lit*)
A luz está apagada.	*The light is switched off.*
O computador está desligado.	*The computer has been turned off.*
As janelas estão fechadas.	*The windows are closed.*
Os portões estão abertos.	*The gates are open.*

Although the verb **engraçar** is not much used, its past participle is handy when you're commenting on something you're looking at:

Isto é engraçado.	*This is funny (amusing).*
Que engraçado!	*How funny!*

Another verb that may come in handy is **combinar**.

Combinado!	*Agreed!*

Insight

Please note that the adjective (or past participle) has to be in the masculine plural where nouns of both genders are being described.

<u>o</u> filh<u>o</u> e <u>a</u> filh<u>a</u> casad<u>os</u>   *the married son and daughter*

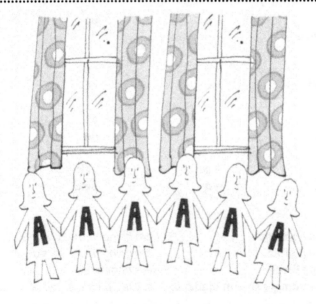

AS JANEL**AS** QUE ESTÃO FECHAD**AS**
TÊM CORTIN**AS** MODERN**AS** E BONIT**AS**.

19 No fim daquela rua, à direita *At the bottom of that road, on your right* (Contracted words and agreement)

You will come across the definite article – o / a (*the*) – in a somewhat disguised appearance. That is because another word has come in and contracted, or combined, with it.

Don't fall into the trap of thinking that Portuguese **no** is a negative. It is a contracted form consisting of **em + o**, and can translate *in*, *on*, etc.

Prepositions (words like *in*, *on*, etc.) are the first element in these combined forms.

Preposition	Definite article	End result
a	+ o	**ao**
to, at, on	+ a	**à**
em	+ o	**no**
in, on	+ a	**na**
de	+ o	**do**
of, from	+ a	**da**
por	+ o	**pelo**
by, for	+ a	**pela**

Eu vou <u>ao</u> campo.	*I am going to the countryside.*
Eu vou <u>à</u> praia.	*I am going to the seaside.*
Ele é <u>do</u> Brasil.	*He is from Brazil.*
Eles moram <u>na</u> ilha <u>da</u> Madeira.	*They live on the island of Madeira.*

| **Entramos sempre <u>pela</u> porta <u>da</u> frente.** | *We always enter by the front door.* |
| **Volto <u>pelas</u> 5 horas.** | *I'll be back around 5 o'clock.* |

Prepositions also contract with the indefinite article and a number of other words that start with a vowel (a, e, i, o, u). These include some pronouns (words used in place of nouns) when they are acting as pronouns or adjectives (a describing or qualifying word) to define something or someone.

Preposition	Other Word	End result
em	+ um / uma	num / numa
em	+ este / esta	neste / nesta
em	+ aquele / aquela	naquele / naquela
em	+ isto	nisto
de	+ este / esta	deste / desta
de	+ aquele / aquela	daquele / daquela
a	+ aquele / aquela	àquele / àquela

Elas moram <u>num</u> bairro moderno.	*They live in a modern residential quarter.*
Eu trabalho <u>nesta</u> empresa.	*I work in this company.*
Nós fomos <u>à</u> casa <u>daquela</u> senhora.	*We went to that lady's house.*
Gosto <u>deste</u> vinho.	*I like this wine.*
Nunca fui <u>àquela</u> praia.	*I have never been to that beach.*

These contracted forms will agree both in gender and number with what they refer to.

Ela é uma <u>das</u> minh<u>as</u> amig<u>as</u>.	*She is one of my friends.*
Ele é <u>dos</u> Estad<u>os</u> Unid<u>os</u>.	*He is from the United States.*
Eles moram <u>numa</u> <u>destas</u> cas<u>as</u>.	*They live in one of these houses.*

20 Meus senhores e minhas senhoras *Ladies and gentlemen* (Possessives and agreement)

Possessives are words that show what belongs to whom – *my, mine, your, yours*, etc. They can be both adjectives, used with a noun (naming word) – <u>*my*</u> *coat* – or pronouns, when they stand for the noun – *mine*.

In Portuguese, both possessive adjectives and pronouns agree in gender (masculine or feminine) and number (singular or plural) with the noun which they refer to, not the owner.

POSSESSIVE ADJECTIVES

Used with a noun (**o casaco**, *coat*; **as luvas**, *gloves*):

Este é <u>o meu</u> casaco.   *This is my coat.* (masculine singular)
Estas são <u>as minhas</u> luvas.   *These are my gloves.* (feminine plural)

POSSESSIVE PRONOUNS

The noun (**o casaco, as luvas**) is not present:

Este é <u>meu</u>.   *This one is mine.* (talking about the coat, masculine singular)
Estas são <u>minhas</u>.   *These (ones) are mine.* (talking about the gloves, feminine plural)

ANOTHER WAY OF SAYING *HIS/HER COAT* AND *GLOVES*

Este é <u>o seu</u> casaco can mean both *This is his/her coat* and *This is your coat*, which can lead to confusion. An alternative for *his/her* is used, particularly in the spoken language.

Este é <u>o casaco d<u>ele</u>.   **dele = de + ele** *(of him)*
This is his coat.

Estas são <u>as</u> luv<u>as</u> d<u>ele</u>.
These are his gloves.
Este é <u>o</u> casac<u>o</u> d<u>ela</u>.   **dela = de + ela** *(of her)*
This is her coat.
Estas são <u>as</u> luv<u>as</u> d<u>ela</u>.
These are her gloves.
Estas são <u>as</u> luv<u>as</u> d<u>eles</u>.   **deles = de + eles** *(of them)* (male)
These are their gloves.
Estes são <u>os</u> casac<u>os</u> del<u>as</u>. **delas = de + elas** *(of them)* (female)
These are their coats.

By the same token:

Este é <u>o</u> d<u>ele</u>.   *This one is his.* (talking about the coat)
Estas são <u>as</u> d<u>ela</u>.   *These (ones) are hers.* (talking about the
                             gloves)
Estes são <u>os</u> d<u>eles</u>. *These (ones) are theirs.* (talking about the
                             men's coats)
Estas são <u>as</u> d<u>elas</u>. *These (ones) are theirs.* (talking about the
                             ladies'gloves)

As you will observe, in this **o(s)/a(s)** (+ noun) **dele(s)/dela(s)**
construction, gender and number grammatical agreement is not
only with the *coat* and the *gloves* but also with whose they are.

21 Esta é uma das minhas malas *This is one of my suitcases* (Possessives with **o/a** and **um/uma**)

'O', 'A', 'OS', 'AS'

In principle, the use of the definite article – **o, a, os, as** – with the possessive is optional. In practice, a lot depends on where you are in the Portuguese-speaking world. A few guidelines should put you on the right track.

In general and particularly at the beginning of a sentence you can say:

Meu pai chegou ontem.   or   **O meu pai chegou ontem.**
My father arrived yesterday.

Both are correct. However, you may find out that a large number of speakers in Brazil will prefer the **meu pai** version and most people in Portugal will say **o meu pai.**

In addition to the general rule above, remember the following:

(A) WHEN TO USE THE DEFINITE ARTICLE WITH THE POSSESSIVE ADJECTIVE

1 When you are being precise about whose is what (*my book*, etc., *no one else's*):

Este é o meu livro.	*This is my book.*
Esta é a minha caneta.	*This is my pen.*

2 When you are using the o(s)/a(s) (+ noun) **dele(s)/dela(s)** expression:

a caneta dele	*his pen*
os livros dela	*her books*
o carro deles	*their car*

(B) WHEN TO USE 'O', 'A', 'OS', 'AS' AS A PRONOUN (*THE ONE*, *THE ONES*) WITH THE POSSESSIVE PRONOUN

When you are being precise about whose is what (*mine*, etc., *no one else's*):

Este é o̲ meu.	*This one is mine.* (book)
Esta é a̲ minha.	*This one is mine.* (pen)

Compare:

Este livro é meu̲.	*This book is mine.* (statement of fact)
Este livro é o̲ meu.	*This book is mine.* (emphatic about possession)

When you are using the o(s)/a(s) dele(s)/dela(s) expression (no noun present):

a̲ dele	*his* (you are talking about his pen)
os̲ dela	*hers* (books)
o̲ deles	*theirs* (car)

Note that the article isn't used when addressing an individual or a group of people directly:

Minhas̲ senhoras e meus̲ senhores   *Ladies and gentlemen (My ladies…)*

'UM', 'UMA', 'UNS', 'UMAS'

Use the indefinite article to translate *a* (+ noun) *of mine*, etc. The um/a etc. can be used together with a noun or on its own as a pronoun.

Encontrei um amigo meu̲ que já não via desde o Natal. (…um meu amigo… is also heard)	*I have met a friend of mine I hadn't seen since Christmas.*
Uma irmã minha̲ está em Angola.	*A sister of mine is (resident) in Angola.*
Estas malas são nossas, umas̲ minhas̲ e outras dele.	*These suitcases are ours, some mine, some (others) his.*

22 Não saia sem o guarda-chuva *Don't go out without your umbrella* (No possessives)

In comparison with other languages, English makes extensive use of the possessives. In some cases, a literal translation into Portuguese would produce a rather nonsensical rendering. A statement like *He drank his milk*, would invite comments such as *Really! He drank his <u>own</u> milk!*

So stay clear of the possessives when ownership is obvious, particularly in the following situations:

(a) Body and mind

Vou lavar <u>as mãos</u>.	*I am going to wash <u>my hands</u>.*
Ele perdeu <u>a perna</u> no desastre.	*He lost <u>his leg</u> in the accident.*
O menino decorou <u>a tabuada</u>.	*The little boy learned <u>his tables</u> by heart.*

(b) Clothing and accessories

Não saia sem pôr <u>o casaco</u>.	*Don't go out without <u>your coat</u> on.*
Você tem alguma coisa <u>no bolso</u>?	*Have you got anything in <u>your pocket</u>?*

(c) Objects for personal use or consumption

Perdi <u>a carteira</u>.	*I have lost <u>my wallet</u>.*
Ele bebeu <u>o leite</u>.	*He drank <u>his milk</u>.*

(d) Professional and occupational equipment

O motorista voltou para <u>o carro</u>.	*The driver went back to <u>his car</u>.*
O médico pegou <u>no estetoscópio</u>.	*The doctor picked up <u>his stethoscope</u>.*

(e) Close family, relations and friends

Ele levou **a filha** para a praia.	He took <u>his daughter</u> to the seaside.
Fomos ao cinema com **os amigos**.	We went to the cinema with <u>our friends</u>.

(f) A pet

Não encontro **o gato**.	I can't find <u>my cat</u>.

All the above examples show a definite article – **a(s)**, **o(s)** – in Portuguese and a possessive adjective – *my, your, his, her*, etc. – in English. In some situations a possessive adjective can also be used in Portuguese, but, since it does not add anything to the basic meaning, it results in adding overtones to it.

Perdi a minha carteira.	I have lost my wallet. (my own)

(It may suggest I was carrying my wallet and someone else's and lost the former.)

Where English uses a possessive adjective to express an action done to, or for, someone, use a personal object pronoun in Portuguese (**me, te, lhe**, etc.)

Ele corta-**me** o cabelo todos os meses.	He cuts <u>my hair</u> every month. (in Portugal)
Ele **me** corta o cabelo todos os meses.	He cuts <u>my hair</u> every month. (in Brazil)

The action doesn't have to been performed by someone else. You can be both the doer and recipient, for example of some injury you have inflicted upon yourself.

Cortei um dedo, mas não me dói.	I have cut my finger, but it does not hurt.

23 Falamos português *We speak Portuguese* (Use and omission of subject pronouns)

You may be overdoing the personal subject pronouns – the words for *I*, *you*, *s/he*, etc. – when you speak or write Portuguese. This can easily happen because you are following the same structure as in English.

In English we need to use *I*, *you*, *s/he*, etc. with the verb to clarify whom or what we are talking about. Their Portuguese counterparts are not always needed because the verb itself often contains this information.

I/WE SPEAK

eu falo
nós falamos

The verb ending '-o' shows that **eu** (*I*) is meant, and the verb ending '-amos' that **nós** (*we*) is meant. As a result, the words **eu** and **nós** are not really needed. The verb itself says it all.

HE/SHE SPEAKS

ele fala
ela fala

As in English, here **ele** or **ela** is needed to know who is speaking.

YOU SPEAK

tu falas (a familiar form of address)
você fala (a general form of address)

In **tu falas** the verb ending '-as' is quite distinctive, so much so that **tu** (*you*) appears to be redundant. In Brazil it is used very little.

In **você fala**, things are a bit different. The verb ending is the same as for *s/he speaks* – **ele** and **ela fala** – which means that **você** (*you*) cannot be omitted as frequently as **tu**.

YOU (MORE THAN ONE) *SPEAK, THEY* (MALE AND FEMALE) *SPEAK*

vocês fal<u>am</u>
eles fal<u>am</u>
elas fal<u>am</u>

All these end in '**-am**', and this means that **vocês, eles, elas** are often needed.

Here are some frequently asked questions:

(1) How do I know when to use the subject pronouns?

Answer: Use them where needed for clarity.

(2) Does this mean that for instance for **fala** I always have to say **você, ele** or **ela**?

Answer: Not necessarily. Context may be enough. If you look at someone and ask: **Fala português?**, it should be obvious that you mean *Do you speak Portuguese?*, not *Does s/he speak Portuguese?*

(3) If I use the subject pronoun where it is not needed, am I making a mistake?

Answer: No, provided you are aware of possible resulting emphasis or overtones.

For instance, you can say either **Falo português** or **Eu falo português**. If you say the latter when some of your colleagues are standing by (particularly if you put some voice stress on the **eu**), it may be understood as *I do speak Portuguese (they don't)*. Overuse of the pronoun may result in the wrong emphasis or overtones rather than a grammatical error.

24a Quem o viu? *Who saw him?* (Object pronouns and word order)

Personal object pronouns – *me, you, him, her, us, them* – are short words without much sound to them. In writing, they tend to be attached to the verb (the doing or being word). In speech they enjoy some freedom within the sentence.

Generally we start with the subject – who or whatever does or is something. Then comes the verb. Next comes the object pronoun, often linked to the verb by a hyphen (-).

Ele viu-me.   *He saw me.*

This basic word order is easily disturbed, for instance, in a negative sentence:

Ele não me viu.   *He didn't see me.*

or in a question started by an interrogative: **onde, quando, como, quanto, quem**, etc.,

Quem me viu?   *Who saw me?*
Onde me viu?   *Where did you see me?*
Quando me viu?   *When did you see me?*

and after words such as **também, ainda, já, enquanto, todos, porque**, etc.

Ele também me viu.   *He saw me too.*
Todos me viram.   *Everybody saw me.*
Ele ainda me viu   *He still saw me before leaving.*
  antes de sair.

The object pronoun no longer follows but precedes the verb. This happens in both the written and spoken language. In the latter the pull towards the beginning of the sentence is even stronger, particularly when more than one verb is involved.

For *Can you tell me where the beach is?* you will hear, in careful speech:

Pode dizer-<u>me</u> onde é a praia?

And more colloquially:

Pode <u>me</u> dizer onde é a praia?

The pull towards the beginning of the sentence is stronger in Brazil than in Portugal and it occurs even when only one verb is involved.

In Brazil you will hear:

Ele <u>me</u> viu.

The same word order pattern applies to the reflexives, which can be classed as an object pronoun where subject and object are one and the same.

In Portugal you will hear:

Eu vesti-<u>me</u>.   *I dressed myself/got dressed.*

In Brazil you are more likely to hear:

Eu <u>me</u> vesti.   *I dressed myself/got dressed.*

While the object and reflexive pronouns appear to have a will of their own in colloquial speech, the basic word order is taken more seriously in the written language and careful speech.

24b Deram-lhe um presente... *They gave him a present...* (More on object pronouns)

A frequent source of confusion in respect of object pronouns is the difference between **o/a** and **lhe**, as they all correspond to *him/her/it/you* in English. So, how does one distinguish them?

A good way is to think of **o/a** as replacing the object or person that 'experiences' the action of the verb.

Lavo o carro.	→	**Lavo-o.**
I wash the car.	→	*I wash it.*
Convido Isabel para a minha festa.	→	**Convido-a para a minha festa.**
I invite Isabel to my party.	→	*I invite her to my party.*
Leste o livro ontem?	→	**Leste-o ontem?**
Did you read the book yesterday?	→	*Did you read it yesterday?*

In all these instances, you can ask '<u>whom</u> or <u>what</u> do/did you wash/invite/read?' The pronoun is replacing that person or thing. For more than one object just add 's': **os/as.**

Li os livros.	→	**Li-os.**
I have read the books.	→	*I have read them.*
Comprou as flores no mercado?	→	**Comprou-as no mercado?**
Did you buy the flowers in the market?	→	*Did you buy them in the market?*
Compraste as maçãs?	→	**Compraste-as?**
Have you bought the apples?	→	*Have you bought them?*

Lhe(s) replaces the person (people) <u>to whom</u> the action is addressed. In Portuguese, this happens mainly with verbs that require the preposition **a** but it is probably easier in English to consider whether you could say do *something <u>to/for</u> someone* – the *someone* is the **lhe**. One small mercy is it has only one form, so there is no need to worry about gender or any other changes!

Examples:

Ofereço um livro ao Paulo.	→	**Ofereço-lhe um livro.**
I give Paulo a book.	→	*I give him a book.*
Telefono à Paula	→	**Telefono-lhe.**
I ring Paula.	→	*I ring her.*

It may be helpful to think of the above as *I give a book to Paulo/ to him* and *I make a call to Paula/to her*.

Other examples:

Peço-lhe.
I ask of you. (or *of him/her* depending on context)
Perguntamos-lhe onde é o banco.
We ask him/her where the bank is, i.e. *We put a question to him/her.*
Disseram-lhes isso ontem.
They said that to them yesterday.

Please don't forget the 'pull' towards the beginning of the sentence in Brazil.

For example, while in Portugal you will hear, as above:

Telefono-lhe.
Perguntamos-lhe onde é o banco.

in Brazil you are more likely to hear:

(Eu) lhe telefono or **(Eu) telefono para ela (Paula).**
(Nós) lhe perguntamos onde é o banco.
(Eles) lhes disseram isso ontem.
(Eu) lhe ofereço um livro.
(Você) as comprou no mercado?

and so on ...

24c ... e deram-no com prazer ... *and they gave it with pleasure* (Even more on object pronouns)

When being introduced to someone, you may have been told:

Muito prazer em **conhecê-lo**. if you are a man or

Muito prazer em **conhecê-la**. if you are a woman

This is an elegant way of saying *Delighted to meet you.* It uses the verb **conhecer**, *to make acquaintance* + **o/a**, *you* (personal object pronoun, masculine/feminine)

Or you may have been invited out using **convidar, + o/a.**

Posso <u>convidá-lo/la</u> para jantar amanhã?   *May I invite you to dinner tomorrow?*

The final '-r' in **conhecer** or **convidar** has jumped over the hyphen and landed as an '-l-' before the **o/a**, while the '-e' or '-a' left behind has received an accent. In the case of **conhecer**, it gains a hat, or, in other words, a circumflex accent (ê):

→ **conhecê-lo/la**

In the case of **convidar,** it gains an acute accent (**á**):

→ **convidá -lo/la.**

This is to keep the original sound of the vowel. The object pronouns **o** and **a** undergo this change (i.e. they become **lo** and **la**) whenever they are after a verb form ending in **-r, -s,** or **-z.**

More examples (this time using **o/a** for *him/her/it*):

Vou levar o menino à escola.	→	**Vou levá-lo à escola.**
I am going to take the little boy to school.	→	*I am going to take him to school.*
Pagamos a conta.	→	**Pagamo-la.**
We pay the bill.	→	*We pay it.*
Traz a gatinha.	→	**Trá-la.**
Bring the kitten (female).	→	*Bring her.*

Similarly, when the verb ends in a nasal sound – **ão, õe, m** – it influences a subsequent **o/a** giving the pronoun an initial **n,** i.e. it becomes **no/na.**

Comprem o livro.	→	**Comprem-no.**
Buy the book.	→	*Buy it.*
Dão a prenda.	→	**Dão-na.**
They give the present.	→	*They give it.*
Põe o carro na garagem.	→	**Põe-no na garagem.**
Put the car in the garage.	→	*Put it in the garage.*

Of course no change takes place when the pronouns come before the verb.

Não pagamos a conta.	→	**Não a pagamos.**
We don't pay the bill.	→	*We don't pay it.*
Ele põe o carro na garagem.	→	**Ele o põe na garagem.** (Brazil)
He puts the car in the garage.	→	*He puts it in the garage.*

Insight

If you can't remember **Muito prazer em conhecê-lo/a,** simply **Muito prazer** will suffice; reply **Igualmente.**

25 Estava calor, mas ontem não esteve *It was hot then, but not yesterday* (Past tenses)

Portuguese sometimes uses a different tense of the verb from the one normally used in English.

HOW MANY DAYS, WEEKS, YEARS?

The Portuguese present indicative, or simple present, can be used to express how long someone has been doing or experiencing something.

Ela está doente desde a semana passada.   *She has been ill since last week.*

Nós moramos aqui há cinco anos.   *We have been living here for five years.*

HOW TO EXPRESS ACTIONS IN THE PAST

This requires a distinction not made in English.

The Portuguese preterite indicative, or past simple, can be used for something completed at some undefined time in the recent past.

Eles chegaram.   *They have arrived.*

Use it too for something finished with, while the imperfect indicative is used for a close-up of something going on in the past.

Esteve calor.   (past simple) *It was hot.* (yesterday, but not today)

Estava calor.   (imperfect) *It was hot.* (over that period of time when I was there)

Also, use:

▶ the preterite, for something that happened in the past when you look at it as a whole.

Trabalhei muito no ano passado.   *I <u>worked</u> hard last year.*
Tomei chá esta manhã.   *I <u>had</u> tea this morning.*

▶ the preterite + imperfect, for something that happened when something else was going on in the past.

Quando eu <u>saí</u>, <u>estava</u> calor.   *When I <u>went</u> out, it <u>was</u> hot.*

▶ the imperfect + imperfect, for something going on in the past at the same time as something else.

Eu <u>lia</u> em voz alta e ele <u>escrevia</u>.
I <u>was reading</u> aloud and he <u>was writing</u>.
Eu <u>passava</u> muito tempo na praia, quando <u>estava</u> calor.
I <u>used to spend</u> a lot of time on the beach, during the hot weather (when it <u>was</u> hot).

USING THE CONDITIONAL

The imperfect often replaces the conditional, particularly in the spoken language.

Eu <u>gostava</u> muito de viajar mais
   frequentemente. (imperfect)
Eu <u>gostaria</u> muito de viajar mais   *I <u>should/would like</u> to travel more*
   frequentemente. (conditional)   *often.*

....
Insight
You can use the imperfect to make polite requests.

Eu <u>queria</u> um café. / <u>Queria</u>   *I <u>would like</u>* (literally, *wanted*)
   um café.   *a coffee.*
<u>Queríamos</u> dois cafés.   *<u>We would like</u> two coffees.*
....

26 Falaremos, quando você vier *We shall talk, when you come* (Future tenses)

English-speaking learners are often misled by a literal interpretation of some Portuguese verb forms used for the future. They are also faced with a verb tense for which there is no direct equivalent in English. As a result, there are instances where you may need to reconfigure the way you express future events and states.

THE *GOING-TO* FUTURE

This tense is formed with **vou, vais, vai,** etc. plus an infinitive. Note that Portuguese infinitives consist of one word which includes the English *to*.

Eu vou comer.   – infinitive **comer**
I am going to eat.   – infinitive *(to) eat*

Here are some more examples. In the first, **Vou ficar** literally means *I go to stay*:

Acho que vou ficar lá uns meses.
I think I am going to stay there for a couple of months.

and **vamos ter** here literally means *we go to have*:

Agora vamos ter mais tempo para fazer tudo.
Now we are going to have more time to do everything.

HOW TO EXPRESS THE NEAR FUTURE IN PORTUGUESE

The Portuguese present simple is often used to express the near future (usually with a time expression to avoid ambiguity).

Eu telefono-te amanhã bem cedo. (Portugal) / **Eu te telefono amanhã bem cedo.** (Brazil)

I am phoning you tomorrow first thing in the morning. or *I will phone you tomorrow first thing in the morning.* (**telefono** literally means I phone)

HOW TO SAY *WHEN, IF,* AND *AS SOON AS* IN PORTUGUESE

When you want to say *when, while* and *as soon as*, the main thing to remember is not to use the present simple as you would in English. First of all you should ask yourself whether what you want to say starts with *when* (**quando**) or *if* (**se**) and refers to something that hasn't happened yet. If this is the case, then you would use the future subjunctive.

As you get the feel of this tense, you can move on to thinking in terms of asking yourself the following: will the action or event I want to express determine the viability or purposefulness of the other action or event I also want to express? If the answer is 'yes', then use the future subjunctive.

Quando você vier amanhã, falaremos.
When you come tomorrow, we shall discuss that. (we shall talk)

In the example above, your being here tomorrow makes it viable for us to discuss the matter.

More examples:

Se eu for a Timor, irei de avião. — *If I go to Timor, I will fly (go by plane).*

Eu ligarei logo que puder. — *I'll phone you as soon as I can.*

Ouvirei tudo quanto você disser. — *I'll listen to everything you say.*

Por favor, fechem a porta quando saírem. — *Please shut the door when you leave.*

Enquanto estivermos aqui, poderemos ir à praia todos os dias. — *While we are staying here, we can go to the beach every day.*

27 Ao sair, encontrei um amigo *As I left, I met a friend* (Personal infinitive)

The infinitive is the basic form of the verb (*to be, walk, think,* etc.) which you will find in a dictionary. A unique feature of Portuguese is the inflected infinitive which gives us more information about the subject of a verb. Study the examples below.

Levo o carro para <u>trazermos</u> as compras.
I take the car for <u>us</u> to bring the shopping.

Sofia, a mãe disse para <u>vires</u> para casa.
Sofia, mother said <u>you</u> should come home / for <u>you</u> to come home.

This construction is so easy that native speakers of Portuguese prefer it to more complex structures involving the subjunctive.

WHAT YOU NEED

You don't need many endings. For the singular persons (*I, you, s/he*) nothing is added unless you use the familiar **tu** approach for *you.* For the plural persons (*we, you, they*), only two different endings are required. The table below shows **comprar** *(to buy)* with the personal endings.

Verb	Person
comprar	**eu,** *I*
compr<u>ares</u>	**tu,** *you* (familiar)
comprar	**você,** *you* (general)
comprar	**ele/ela,** *he/she*
comprar<u>mos</u>	**nós,** *we*
comprar<u>em</u>	**vocês,** *you* (more than one)
comprar<u>em</u>	**eles/elas,** *they* (masculine/feminine)

Where there is no ending – *I, you (*general*), s/he* – or a shared ending – *you* (more than one), *they* – the personal subject pronoun word – **eu, você, ele /ela, vocês, eles / elas** – may be needed for clarity.

HOW TO USE IT

Let's start with examples that have a relatively close English translation, and then gradually move away.

Eles pediram para <u>cantarmos</u>. (**cantar,** *to sing*)
They asked us to sing.

É importante <u>compreendermos</u> o infinitivo pessoal. (**compreender,** *to understand*)
It is important for us to understand the personal infinitive.

É necessário <u>ele estudar</u> um pouco todos os dias. (**estudar,** *to study*)
He must study a little every day.

Sem <u>eles verem</u>, abri a porta. (**ver,** *to see*)
Without them seeing it, I opened the door.

Depois de <u>eu entrar</u> em casa, eles telefonaram. (**entrar,** *to enter, walk in*)
After my entering the house, they phoned./After I had walked in, they phoned.

Ao <u>chegar</u>, vá diretamente para a reunião. (**chegar,** *to arrive*)
On arriving, go straight to the meeting./As soon as you arrive, go to the meeting.

Comprei este livro para <u>você</u> o <u>ler</u>. (**ler,** *to read*)
I bought this book for you to read. / so that you can/may read it.

Eu tinha comprado o livro para <u>ele</u> o <u>ler</u>. (**ler,** *to read*)
I had bought the book for him to read. / so that he could/might read it.

28 Faz muito sol *It is very sunny* (Impersonal sentences)

Impersonal sentences are common in both English and Portuguese. They draw attention to the action rather than the person carrying it out and can be both singular and plural. Study the following examples:

Singular:

<u>Está</u> vermelho. *It's red.*

Plural:

<u>Dizem</u> que essa planta é venenosa. *That plant is supposed to be poisonous.* (literally, (*They*) *say that that plant is poisonous.*)

You can use impersonal sentences to talk about the following:

THE WEATHER

Chove.	*It rains.*	(verb **chover**)
Neva.	*It snows.*	(verb **nevar**)
Chove muito.	*It rains a lot.*	

The verb **fazer** can also be used without an expressed agent.

Faz sol.	*It is sunny.*
Faz frio.	*It is cold.*
Faz calor.	*It is hot.*
Faz muito calor.	*It is very hot.*

The same applies when talking about past weather...

Fez calor.	*It was hot.* (yesterday, not today)
Fazia calor.	*It was hot.* (at that time I was talking about)
Esteve calor.	*It was hot.* (yesterday, not today)

Estava calor.	*It was hot.* (at that time I was talking about)
Chovia muito.	*It was raining a lot.* (at that time I was talking about)

... or when predicting or speculating about future weather.

Amanhã vai chover.	*It is going to rain tomorrow.*
Fará calor amanhã?	*Will it be hot tomorrow?*

PAIN, USING 'DOER', *TO HURT*

This may be useful if you have to see a doctor or tell someone you are not feeling well. It has only two forms:

dói (if what hurts is one thing)
doem (if what hurts is plural, e.g. teeth)

Dói aqui.	*It hurts here.*
Dói muito.	*It hurts a lot.*

It can also be accompanied by an indirect object pronoun.

dói-me ... (Portugal)
me dói ... (Brazil)

... **a cabeça.**	*my head hurts.*
... **a mão.**	*my hand hurts.*
... **o pé.**	*my foot hurts.*

doem-me ... (Portugal)
me doem ... (Brazil)

... **os dentes.**	*my teeth hurt.*
... **as costas.** (note the plural)	*my back hurts.*

Now that you know how to handle Portuguese impersonal sentences, you'll find them as easy as in English!

29 Está-se bem neste hotel *It is comfortable at this hotel* (The **se** format and its roles)

Portuguese uses reflexives (where subject and object are the same) much more widely than English. It also uses the reflexive format for other purposes.

REFLEXIVE 'SE' *(ONESELF)*

In a limited number of cases there is coincidence of practice between Portuguese and English, for example **ver-se:**

Eu <u>vi-me</u> no espelho. (Portugal) / **Eu <u>me vi</u> no espelho.** (Brazil)
I saw myself in the mirror.

A reflexive translation may be found in English but it tends not to be first choice. For instance **divertir-se** and **sentar-se:**

Eles <u>divertiram-se</u> na festa. (Portugal) / **Eles <u>se divertiram</u> na festa.** (Brazil)
They amused themselves. / They had a good time at the party.

A senhora <u>sentou-se</u> na cadeira. (Portugal) / **A senhora <u>se sentou</u> na cadeira.** (Brazil)
The lady sat (herself) on the chair.

It makes good sense. After all,

A senhora <u>sentou a criança</u> na cadeira. *The lady sat the child on the chair.*

But you would normally say in English, *The lady sat down on the chair.*

In fact mostly Portuguese and English renderings are quite different, for example **chamar-se:**

Eu <u>chamo-me</u> João. (Portugal) / **Eu <u>me chamo</u> João.** (Brazil)
My name is João.

Similarly, **levantar-se** *(to get up)*, **despedir-se** *(to say goodbye)*, **esquecer-se** *(to forget)*, **lembrar-se** *(to remember)* and **casar-se** *(to get married)*.

RECIPROCAL 'SE' – EACH OTHER

Se expressions are also used for a reciprocal action. Here there is a fairly straightforward parallel in English, for example **amar-se** and **compreender-se**:

Eles <u>amam-se</u> muito. (Portugal) / **Eles <u>se amam</u> muito.** (Brazil)
They love each other dearly.

Eles <u>compreendem-se</u>. (Portugal) / **Eles <u>se compreendem</u>.** (Brazil)
They understand one another.

IMPERSONAL 'SE' THE PASSIVE, ONE DOES, PEOPLE DO

These are also three frequent English renderings for **se** expressions.

Aqui <u>fala-se</u> Português. (falar-se)	*Portuguese is spoken here.*
<u>**Vende-se**</u> **(vender-se)**	*To be sold/For sale*
No verão <u>vai-se</u> muito à praia. **(ir-se)**	*In summer one goes/people go quite a lot to the beach.*
<u>**Está-se**</u> **bem neste hotel.** **(estar-se)**	*One is (made to feel) comfortable at this hotel /It's comfortable at this hotel.*

> Portuguese normal rendering
> **Eu chamo-me Laura.** (Portugal) / **Eu me chamo Laura**. (Brazil).
> ↓
> *I call myself Laura.*
> ↓
> *I am called Laura.*
> ↓
> ***My name is Laura.***
> English normal rendering

Try to work your way in reverse and you should find a safe route to the right rendering in Portuguese.

30 Como é que você se chama? *What's your name?* (É que and word order)

Now it is time to get your word order right with a little help from é que.

é que (literally *(it) is + that*) are filler words that can help you with word order sequence on both sides of the Atlantic.

Onde você mora? (Brazil) / **Onde mora você?** (Portugal)
    subject + verb   verb + subject
Where do you live?

but

Onde é que você mora? (Brazil and Portugal)
         subject + verb

Similarly,

Como se chama você? (Portugal) / **Como você se chama?** (Brazil)
What is your name? (literally, *How do you call yourself?*)

but

Como é que você se chama? (Portugal and Brazil)
What is your name? (literally, *How do you call yourself?*)

Quantos anos tem você? (Portugal) / **Quantos anos você tem?**
 (Brazil)
How old are you? (literally, *How many years have you got?*)

but

Quantos anos é que você tem? (Portugal and Brazil)
How old are you? (literally, *How many years have you got?*)

Please note that this is applicable in questions starting with a question word – **onde** (*where*), **como** (*how*), **quantos** (*how many*), **quando** (*when*), **o que** (*what*) etc.

Quando é que vocês vão?	*When do you go?*
O que é que tu compraste?	*What did you buy?*

You don't need it in questions such as the ones below which do not belong in the above category.

<u>**Você é**</u> **português?**	*Are you Portuguese?*	(asking a man)
<u>**Você é**</u> **portuguesa?**	*Are you Portuguese?*	(asking a woman)
<u>**Você é**</u> **brasileiro?**	*Are you Brazilian?*	(asking a man)
<u>**Você é**</u> **brasileira?**	*Are you Brazilian?*	(asking a woman)

31 Vocês gostam de música, não gostam? *You like music, don't you?* (Tag questions)

In conversation, we often add a question phrase to a statement, to seek confirmation or agreement: *He is here, isn't he? It isn't a fine day today, is it?* English has two kinds of question tag. In the first, the verb from the statement is repeated:

You can speak Portuguese, <u>can't</u> you?

You didn't walk here, <u>did</u> you?

He won't phone, <u>will</u> he?

You haven't bought a car, <u>have</u> you?

You are going to the party, <u>aren't</u> you?

In the second, *don't you*, etc. is added at the end of the sentence:

You want to go shopping, <u>don't</u> you?

They went to the beach yesterday, <u>didn't</u> they?

The aeroplane arrived late, <u>didn't</u> it?

You like music, <u>don't</u> you?

You will have a problem if you try to translate all this literally into Portuguese. On the other hand, if you go about Portuguese question tags the Portuguese way, you will find out they couldn't be easier. In (A) and (B) below you will find a Portuguese solution for the different English question tags shown above.

(A) QUESTION TAG FOR AN AFFIRMATIVE STATEMENT

Repeat the verb exactly as in the statement but preceded by **não**.

Ele está cá, não está?
He is here, isn't he?

Você sabe falar Português, não sabe?
You can speak Portuguese, can't you?

Vocês vão à festa, não vão?
You are going to the party, aren't you?

Você quer ir fazer compras, não quer?
You want to go shopping, don't you?

Eles foram à praia ontem, não foram?
They went to the beach yesterday, didn't they?

O avião chegou atrasado, não chegou?	*The aeroplane arrived late, didn't it?*
Vocês gostam de música, não gostam?	*You like music, don't you?*

Or simply use the all-purpose expression **não é?** (*isn't it?, aren't you?, didn't they?*, etc.), more so in Brazil than in Portugal.

Ele está cá, não é?	*He is here, isn't he?*
Vocês gostam de música, não é?	*You like music, don't you?*

(B) QUESTION TAG FOR A NEGATIVE STATEMENT

In Portugal simply use **pois não?** and in Brazil, **não é?**:

Hoje não está um dia bonito, pois não?	*It isn't a fine day today, is it?*
Você não veio a pé, pois não?	*You didn't walk here, did you?*
Você não comprou um carro, não é?	*You haven't bought a car, have you?*
Ele não vai telefonar, não é?	*He won't phone, will he?*

(C) RESPONSE TO THE TAG QUESTION

You can just reply **sim** (*yes*) or **não** (*no*). For a more elaborate reply, you can choose from the following options:

▶ Verb repetition and **Pois não?** question tags: repeat the sentence verb, for the appropriate person:

Ele <u>está</u> cá, não está?	
(Sim,) está.	**(Não,) não está.**
Você <u>sabe</u> falar Português, não sabe?	
(Sim,) sei. ... *I can*	**(Não,) não sei.** ... *I can't*
Você não <u>veio</u> a pé, pois não?	
(Sim,) vim. ... *I did*	**(Não,) não vim.** ... *I didn't*

▶ **Não é?** question tags (mostly Brazil): just say **(Sim)** é/**(Não)** não é.

32 Vamos para casa pelo parque *We are going home through the park* (Prepositions **para** and **por**)

Para and **por** are two prepositions that have probably caused you a few headaches. Apart from sounding similar they both often translate the English *for*. How do you decide which to choose? Before we look at some rules and examples, you will need to remind yourself of the contraction of **por** with the articles (see Chapter 19): **por** + **o**(s) = **pelo**(s) and **por** + **a**(s) = **pela**(s). This is particularly important because what appears in some of the examples below is not **por** but **pelo** or **pela**.

'PARA'

(a) **Para** looks to the future, the end of the action; it expresses destination, purpose, objective. It translates *to* or *towards* in most instances, though it can also correspond to *for*.

É tarde, vou <u>para</u> casa.	*It's late, I'm going home.*
Ele avançou <u>para</u> a janela quando ouviu o barulho <u>para</u> ver o que se passava.	*He moved towards the window to see what was happening when he heard the noise.*
Este livro é <u>para</u> alunos de Português.	*This book is for students of Portuguese.*

(b) **Para** can also express a deadline (usually combined with **pronto**), or a time.

O professor quer os exercícios prontos <u>para</u> amanhã.	*The teacher wants the exercises ready for/by tomorrow.*
A reunião foi adiada <u>para</u> 4ª feira.	*The meeting was postponed to Wednesday.*

'POR'

(a) **Por** often shows the origin, the cause or the means of an action. It translates *by*, *because of*, *on account of* or sometimes *for*.

Faltei à aula <u>por</u> doença.	*I missed the lesson because of illness.*
Levei o seu livro <u>por</u> não ter aqui o meu.	*I took your book because I didn't have mine here.*
Parabéns <u>pelas</u> boas notas.	*Congratulations on your good marks. (exam results)*

(b) When relating to movement, **por** also means *through* or *near by* (usually with **passar**).

Vamos <u>pelo</u> parque. O caminho é mais longo mas é mais agradável.	*Let's go through the park. The way is longer but it's more pleasant.*
Iremos passar <u>por lá</u>.	*We shall be going that way.*

(c) When relating to time, **por** means an approximate time (which can be represented by a festival or an occasion) or a period of time.

O Dr. Santos deve estar em casa <u>pelas</u> 7h.	*Dr Santos should be home around 7 o'clock.*
<u>Pela</u> Páscoa vamos acampar.	*At Easter, we'll go camping.*
Queria alugar o carro <u>por</u> 10 dias.	*I'd like to hire the car for 10 days.*
No verão, o Diogo e a Telma vão para o Algarve <u>por</u> um mês.	*In the summer, Diogo and Telma go to the Algarve for a month.*

(d) Finally, **por** also conveys the idea of exchange.

Este casaco está muito apertado; vou trocar <u>por</u> outro.	*This jacket is too tight; I'm going to exchange it for another.*
Paguei €4 <u>pela</u> melancia.	*I paid €4 for the watermelon.*

33 Fui de carro e também a cavalo *I went by car and also on horseback* (Prepositions **de** and **a**)

The prepositions **de** and **a** are often a source of confusion to people whose mother tongue is English. Let's now look at how they are used.

▶ Means of transport are preceded by **de**:

Eles vieram de avião.   *They came by plane.*

except when you make the vehicle specific (when you use **em**):

Fomos no carro do Pedro.   *We went in Pedro's car.*

and also except for **a** cavalo and **a** pé:

Gosto muito de andar a cavalo. *I like horse riding very much.*
Vou a pé para o escritório. *I go to the office on foot.*

▶ De can mean *of*, *from* or *about* as in the following examples:

A capital de Portugal é Lisboa. *The capital of Portugal is Lisbon.*
Venho de Lisboa. *I come from Lisbon.*
Ele falou de Lisboa. *He spoke about Lisbon.*

▶ Both **a** and **para** are used to indicate destination – **a** suggesting a going and returning action.

Para is used for one-way trips and also when you only want to state the destination irrespective of how long you are staying there and whether you are coming back. Thus, when you say

Agora vamos para casa da Maria

you are not interested in anything that happens afterwards. But with

Agora vamos a casa da Maria

you are implying that you are only popping over, you are not staying there.

▶ Other uses of a:

1 In the following expressions:

à esquerda / direita	*on the left / right*
ao norte / sul	*to the North / South*
ao lado de / ao pé de	*next to*
ao sol / à sombra / à chuva	*in the sun / shade / rain*

Não estejas ao sol sem chapéu!	*Don't be in the sun without*
Ficas doente.	*a hat! You'll be ill.*

2 For approximate distances:

A escola do Miguel é muito perto.	*Miguel's school is nearby. It's*
Fica a 100 m (fica a 5 minutos).	*100 m (it's 5 minutes) away.*

3 For prices:

As laranjas são a €3 o quilo.	*The oranges cost €3 per kilo.*

Insight

Notice that:
Em pé / de pé means *standing* not *on foot*.

Choosing the right words

34a Ele é do Rio de Janeiro *He is from Rio de Janeiro* (Ways of saying 'to be')

When you look up *be* (*to be*) in an English-Portuguese dictionary, you are given both **ser** and **estar**. It may be a bit tricky when it comes to decide which to select. For the right choice ask yourself: Am I defining or characterizing something or someone? If your answer is *yes*, you will need **ser**. **Ser** is used to express the following inherent conditions:

▶ general statements and impersonal expressions:

O gelo é frio.	*Ice is cold.*

▶ specifying something:

Que é isto? É uma carta.	*What is this? It's a letter.*

▶ a permanent location (countries, towns, buildings):

O Brasil é na América do Sul.	*Brazil is in South America.*
A Torre de Belém é um dos monumentos mais célebres de Portugal.	*The Tower of Belém is one of Portugal's most famous monuments.*

▶ numbers, quantity, time and dates:

Cinco e cinco são dez.	*5 and 5 are 10.*
Quanto é?	*How much is it?*
São 3 horas.	*It is 3 o'clock.*

▶ place of origin/nationality:

Você é americano?	*Are you American?*

▶ physical or character traits:

Ele é alto.	*He is tall.*

- ▶ personal relationships which are unchangeable:

  Nós <u>somos</u> pai e filho.   *We are father and son.*

- ▶ marital status and relationships perceived as unchangeable:

  <u>Sou</u> casada.   *I am married. (a married woman)*

- ▶ professions and occupations:

  Nós <u>somos</u> estudantes.   *We are students.*

- ▶ the material which something is made from, followed by **de**:

  Isto <u>é</u> de plástico.   *This is (made of) plastic.*

- ▶ climate (as an identifying feature):

  O clima de Lisboa <u>é</u> ameno.   *Lisbon has a mild climate.*

- ▶ colour (as a distinguishing feature):

  O limão <u>é</u> amarelo.   *Lemons are yellow in colour.*

- ▶ belonging, followed by **de**:

  Estas revistas <u>são</u> do João.   *These magazines are João's.*

- ▶ pointing out someone or something:

  <u>Sou</u> eu.   *It's me.*

- ▶ identifying someone or something by a dominant feature:

  <u>É</u> difícil.   *It's (something is) difficult.*

Like **ser, ficar** can be used to indicate permanent location:

     O Brasil <u>fica</u> na América do Sul.   *Brazil is in South America.*

34b Ela está de férias no Algarve *She is on holiday in the Algarve* (More ways of saying 'to be')

In 34a we looked at examples where you need **ser** when translating English *to be*. Now ask yourself the following question: Am I talking about a feature that can change easily? if the answer is *yes*, you will need **estar**. Estar is used for conditions which are not inherent:

▶ location of movables including people:

O livro está em cima da mesa.	*The book is on the table.*
Aqui está a chave.	*Here is your key.*
Estamos em casa.	*We are at home. (at this moment)*

▶ a temporary situation:

Estou de férias.	*I am on holiday.*

▶ the weather:

Hoje está frio.	*Today it is cold.*

▶ physical and mental states, mood:

Estou muito cansada.	*I am very tired.*
Estás contente?	*Are you happy?*
Estou com sede.	*I am thirsty.*

Insight

Ter can be used as an alternative to **estar com**:

Estou com sede. / Tenho sede.	*I am thirsty. (lit I am with thirst and I have thirst)*
Tenho pressa. / Estou com pressa.	*I am in a hurry.*
Tenho medo. / Estou com medo.	*I am frightened.*

A choice of **ser** or **estar** may depend on the speaker's outlook.

Ela <u>é</u> divorciada.	*She is a divorcée/She is divorced.*
Ela <u>está</u> divorciada.	*She has divorced.*
Ele <u>é</u> aposentado.	*He is a retired man.*
Ele <u>está</u> aposentado.	*He has retired.*

For different meanings, **ser** or **estar** can be contrasted.

Esta sala <u>é</u> bonita.	*This room looks nice.*
Esta sala <u>está</u> bonita.	*This room is looking quite nice.* (as a result of some improvement)
Aquele rapaz <u>é</u> alto.	*That boy is tall.*
Aquele rapaz <u>está</u> alto.	*That boy has been growing fast.*
Ela <u>é</u> alegre.	*She is of a cheerful disposition.*
Ela <u>está</u> alegre.	*She is in a happy mood.*

Now you should be more than well equipped to distinguish between **ser** and **estar** and may even have come to the conclusion that it's quite easy.

To summarize:

Inherent	Not inherent
<u>Sou</u> de Lisboa	<u>Estou</u> num hotel
português	de passagem
engenheiro	com pressa
solteiro	cansado
alto	
I am from Lisbon	*I am* staying at an hotel
Portuguese	passing through
an engineer	in a hurry
single	tired
tall	

35 Ela tem trinta anos *She is thirty years old*
(Other expressions of being)

In some situations where you would use the verb *to be* in English, you would use **ter, fazer** or **ficar** in Portuguese.

Study the sentences below where a mother is talking about her daughter's age and birthday. What is she saying?

Agora ela <u>tem</u> dez anos. *Now she <u>is</u> ten years old.* **(ter)**
Ela <u>fez</u> dez anos ontem. *She <u>was</u> ten years old yesterday.* **(fazer)**
Ela <u>ficou</u> muito contente *She <u>was</u> very happy with the* **(ficar)**
com os presentes que *presents she received.*
recebeu.

PARABÉNS A VOCÊ,
NESTA DATA QUERIDA,
MUITA FELICIDADE,
MUITOS ANOS DE VIDA.
*

* LYRICS BY
BERTHA CELESTE
HOMEM DE
MELLO, A LADY
FROM BRAZIL.
SUNG TO
THE MUSIC
OF
HAPPY
BIRTHDAY.

You can express age either by using **ter** or **fazer**.

TER

(Eu) <u>tenho</u> vinte e cinco anos.   *I am 25 years old.*
<u>Tenho</u> setenta anos.   *I am 70 years old.*

Note: **Tenho 25/70 anos** (literally, *I have 25/70 years*, in the sense *I have completed 25/70 years of age*).

FAZER

(Eu) <u>fiz</u> quarenta anos ontem.   *I was forty years old yesterday.*
Quando <u>fiz</u> 25 anos...   *When I had my twenty-fifth birthday...*

Note: **fiz 25/40/70 anos** (literally, *I made 25/40/70 years*, in the sense *I reached 25/40/70 years of age*).

FICAR AND ESTAR

Ficar can be used in preference to **estar** to express a state or situation.

(Eu) <u>estou</u> cansada.   *I am tired.*   (**estar**)
but
(Eu) <u>fiquei</u> cansada depois da festa.   *I was tired after the party.*   (**ficar**)

<u>Fiquei</u> muito contente com   *I was very happy with the*
os presentes que vocês me   *presents you brought me.*
trouxeram.

Note: **fiquei contente ...** (literally, *I was happy*, in the sense *I became happy as a result of ...*)

> ## Insight
> **<u>Tenho</u> 25 anos.**   *I am 25 years old.*
> **<u>Fiz</u> 25 anos ontem.**   *I was 25 yesterday.*
> **<u>Fiquei</u> contente com a festa.**   *I enjoyed my party.* (was happy with it)

36 Tomo café todos os dias *I have coffee every day* (Not 'to have')

'TER' = *TO HAVE*

In its core meaning, Portuguese **ter** translates *to have*:

Eles <u>têm</u> dois carros.	*They <u>have</u> two cars.* (they own them)

But *to have* is used quite extensively and beyond the concept of possession and ownership in English. You, therefore, need to pay careful attention to the context to decide which verb to use in Portuguese.

(A) FOOD AND DRINK

Use verbs (action words) **tomar** or **beber**, for something you drink, and **comer** for something you eat.

I <u>have</u> coffee every day.	**<u>Tomo</u> café todos os dias.**
I am going to <u>have</u> a glass of water.	**Vou <u>beber</u> um copo de água.**

(B) MEALS

Tomar is used for breakfast, but not for other meals.

<u>Tomo</u> sempre o pequeno-almoço antes de sair de casa. (Portugal)
<u>Tomo</u> sempre o café (da manhã) antes de sair de casa. (Brazil)
I always <u>have</u> breakfast before leaving home.

Almoçar, jantar, lanchar

<u>Almoçamos</u> na cantina todos os dias.	*We <u>have</u> lunch in the canteen every day.*
Nunca <u>lancho</u>.	*I never <u>have</u> afternoon tea. / a snack mid-afternoon.*
Vocês <u>jantaram</u> com a Leonor?	*Did you <u>have</u> dinner with Leonor?*

(C) PERSONAL CARE (HYGIENE, MEDICAL, ETC.)

Both **tomar** and **fazer** are frequently used.

Gosto de <u>tomar</u> banho antes de me deitar.	*I like <u>having</u> a bath before going to bed.*
<u>Tomou</u> o remédio?	*Have you <u>had</u> your medicine?*
Ela <u>fez</u> uma operação.	*She <u>had</u> an operation.*

(D) OTHER VERBS USED IN THE SENSE OF *TO HAVE.*

<u>Fizemos</u> uma festa. (fazer)	*We <u>had</u> a party.*
<u>Mandei</u> fazer isto para ela. (clothes, etc.) **(mandar)**	*I <u>had</u> this made for her.*
Eles <u>divertiram-se</u>. (Portugal)/ **<u>Se divertiram</u>.** (Brazil)	*They <u>had</u> a good time.* (literally, they enjoyed themselves)

(E) *I'LL HAVE …, PLEASE*

When ordering something in a café or restaurant, instead of saying *I'll have a coffee and a cake*, you simply say:

Um café e um bolo, por favor.
(Eu) queria um café e um bolo.
Para mim, um café e um bolo.

Now you are ordering coffee and cake, for yourself, and mineral water and a passion fruit sorbet, for your lady friend:

Um café, uma água mineral, um bolo e um sorvete de maracujá.
(Nós) queríamos café, uma água mineral, um bolo e um sorvete de maracujá.
Para mim um café e um bolo, e para a senhora, uma água mineral e um sorvete de maracujá.

....
Insight
If you translate literally *I'll have a coffee* – **Terei um café** – that may suggest you are hoping to become a café owner!
....

37 Há mesas livres? *Are there any tables available?* ('There is', 'there are' and more)

This unit deals with **há,** a useful and important expression. It is important to get this right.

Há is a form of the verb **haver** and you are probably familiar with it as an alternative to **tem.** For instance, in a restaurant you can ask

Há mesas livres?	instead of	**Tem mesas livres?**
Are there/have you got any tables available?		

or in a shop

Há laranjas hoje?	equivalent to	**Tem laranjas hoje?**
Have you got any oranges today?		

or you may have been told

Já não há o Times.	for	**Já não temos o Times.**
No Times left; sold out.		

You have probably already noticed that, in the above examples, **há** is used with both one thing or many. It means *there is* or *there are*.

Examples:

Desculpe, há um banco perto?	*Excuse me, is there a bank nearby?*
Há hotéis bons nesta cidade?	*Are there any good hotels in this town?*
Há um programa interessante na televisão hoje à noite.	*There is an interesting programme on television tonight.*
Há restaurantes típicos na praia.	*There are some typical restaurants on the beach.*
Há nevoeiro no rio e por isso os barcos estão parados.	*There is fog on the river so the boats are not running.*

Note that, where in English you might ask *Are there any* ... or say *There are some* ..., in Portuguese it is only **Há** ....

You can also use the preterite and the imperfect of **haver** (**houve** and **havia,** respectively) for *there was/were.*

Houve um acidente aqui ontem.	*There was an accident here yesterday.*
Antigamente havia uma fonte na praça.	*In the old days there was a fountain in the square.*
Havia muitos alunos na minha escola.	*There were many pupils in my school.*

Há, however, has a completely different meaning when combined with expressions of time.

1 It means *for* with the verb in the present.

Vivo em Inglaterra há 20 anos.	*I've been living in England for 20 years.*
Há quanto tempo é que você estuda Português?	*For how long have you been studying Portuguese?*
Não vamos ao cinema há 6 meses.	*We haven't been to the cinema for 6 months.*

2 It means *ago* with the verb in the past.

Falei com o Diogo há 3 dias.	*I spoke to Diogo 3 days ago.*
Eles partiram há meia hora.	*They left half an hour ago.*
Ele telefonou há 10 minutos.	*He rang 10 minutes ago.*
Fomos ao Brasil há 2 anos.	*We went to Brazil 2 years ago.*

38 Mil, cento e trinta e duas pessoas *One thousand, one hundred and thirty-two people* (Numerals)

Pay careful attention to some of these points about the use of cardinal numbers (*one*, *two*, *three*, etc.).

▶ In Portuguese, number *one* has two forms, **um** for masculine and **uma** for feminine.

<u>um</u> alun<u>o</u>	*one student (male student)*
<u>uma</u> alun<u>a</u>	*one student (female student)*

▶ The same applies for *two*, **dois** for masculine and **duas** for feminine.

<u>dois</u> alun<u>os</u>	*two students (male)*
<u>duas</u> alun<u>as</u>	*two students (female)*

▶ After **cem** (*one hundred*), any combination of 100 plus tens or units results in a change to **cento** (*a hundred*).

<u>cento</u> e um/a	*one/a hundred and one*
<u>cento</u> e quinze	*one/a hundred and fifteen*

▶ English *a* is not translated before **cem**, **cento** or **mil** (*thousand*).

<u>cem</u> euros	*a hundred euros*
<u>cento</u> e vinte libras	*a hundred and twenty pounds*
<u>mil</u> dólares	*a thousand dollars*

▶ The word **e** appears between hundreds, tens and units.

cento <u>e</u> vinte <u>e</u> três	*one/a hundred and twenty-three*

▶ Starting at two hundred and up to nine hundred, cardinals have a masculine and a feminine form.

duzent<u>os</u> alun<u>os</u>	*two hundred students (male)*
novecent<u>as</u> alun<u>as</u>	*nine hundred students (female)*
quinhent<u>as</u> e vinte e du<u>as</u>	*five hundred and twenty-two*
alun<u>as</u>	* students (female)*

▶ Numbers over one thousand are always expressed in thousands and hundreds, not as multiples of a hundred.

mil e quatrocentos	*one thousand four hundred =*
	fourteen hundred = 1400

▶ The word e appears after thousands:

1 When the thousand is followed directly by a numeral from 1–100:

oito mil <u>e</u> noventa e quatro	*8,094*

2 When the thousand is followed by a numeral from 200–999, if the last two numbers are zeros.

quarenta mil <u>e</u> quinhentos	*40,500*

▶ A full stop, not a comma, is used after thousands, etc.

1.500	*1,500*
250.930	*250,930*

As an alternative you can leave a thin space.

1 500	*1,500*
250 930	*250,930*

▶ A comma, not a full stop, is used to mark the decimal point.

A temperatura ontem chegou	*The temperature yesterday*
aos 25,8˚C.	* reached 25.8˚C.*

The temperature would be read out on television or radio as: ... vinte e cinco <u>vírgula</u> oito graus).

39 São vinte e cinco de junho *It's 25 June* (Dates)

Dates are not difficult in Portuguese and yet this is an area where mistakes often occur. So let's look at a few basic points.

(A) DAYS AND MONTHS

Cardinal numbers (*one*, *two*, etc.) are used for the days of the month.

dezoito de fevereiro / 18 de fevereiro	*the eighteenth of February*

The ordinal (*first*) can be used for the first day of the month:

o primeiro de janeiro / o 1˚ de Janeiro	*the first of January*

(B) 'É' OR 'SÃO' (WITH DATES)?

São is the verb form used (verb **ser**) for all days of the month except the first day.

hoje é (o) primeiro de maio	*today it is the first of May*
hoje são treze de julho	*today it is the thirteenth of July*

(C) YEARS

For years over 1000 you cannot omit **mil** as is often done in English.

mil e novecentos	*nineteen hundred (1900)*
mil, setecentos e doze	*seventeen hundred and twelve (1712)*
dois mil	*two thousand (2000)*
dois mil e dez	*two thousand and ten (2010)*

(D) WRITING DATES

When writing the year in the date (as you would at the beginning of a letter), a **de** goes between the month and the year.

22 de abril <u>de</u> 2010   *22nd of April 2010*

Abbreviated dates may appear with the day of the month first and the year last or vice versa.

<u>22</u>/04/10 or **<u>10</u>/04/22 = 22 de abril de 2010**

(E) CENTURIES

Early centuries can be expressed in ordinals, but from the tenth onwards cardinals are preferred.

no <u>primeiro</u> século d.C.   *in the first century* AD
  (depois de Cristo)
no século <u>vinte e um</u>   *in the twenty-first century*

(F) HOW TO SAY DATES ALOUD

When reading aloud dates expressed in numbers use a cardinal (1, 2, etc.), not an ordinal (1st, 2nd, etc.) for the month. Retain the **de** both between the day and the month and between the month and the year, the first one appearing as **do** (= **de** + **o**) where **o** stands for month, **o mês**.

25/12/89 = 25 do 12 de 89
vinte e cinco <u>do</u> doze <u>de</u>   *twenty-fifth of the twelfth,*
  oitenta e nove   *eighty-nine*

(For lower numbers you may also come across **do** for the year – 22 do 4 do 10.)

40 De segunda a sexta-feira *From Monday to Friday* (Weekdays)

Portuguese has a distinctive way of naming the days of the week. Weekdays – Monday to Friday – are expressed by using ordinal numbers followed by the word **feira**. This tends to be an area of uncertainty, and there are some frequently asked questions.

- ▶ Why are the weekdays numbered?
- ▶ Why is Monday the *second day*?
- ▶ Why is Tuesday **terça**, not **terceira**?

If you find the days of the week confusing, there is no better solution than finding out how their names originate.

Pagan names for the days of the week were adopted in English and other European languages, e.g. *Monday*, meaning *the day of the Moon* and *Sunday*, meaning *the day of the Sun*. In Portuguese though, the days were named according to the Christian week.

The first *holy* day was Sunday, **prima feria**. It was the *day of the Lord*, the day for going to church. Its name was later changed to **domenica**, today **domingo**. Saturday is today's **sábado** derived from *sabbath*. Between these two days, we have the ordinals, from second to sixth, followed by the word **feira**, a linguistic corruption of original **feria**.

The reason why **terça**, not **terceira**, is used for Tuesday is simply because the word for *third* has taken a shortened form.

Please also note that no (initial) capital letter is used:

domingo	*Sunday*	**quinta-feira**	*Thursday*
segunda-feira	*Monday*	**sexta-feira**	*Friday*
terça-feira	*Tuesday*	**sábado**	*Saturday*
quarta-feira	*Wednesday*		

▶ You may hear the days of the week in the singular or plural.

Para mim, <u>as segundas-feiras</u> são   *For me, Mondays are*
sempre dias muito ocupados.   *always rather busy days.*
Para mim, <u>(a) segunda-feira</u> é   *For me, Monday is always*
sempre um dia muito ocupado.   *a rather busy day.*

▶ The word **feira** is often dropped in colloquial speech and transport timetables.

Eu vou lá na próxima <u>terça</u>.   *I am going there next Tuesday.*

▶ Both **a** and **em** are used with the days of the week – with the resulting forms **ao(s)/à(s)** (= a + o/a(s)) and **no(s)/na(s)** (= em + o/a(s)) – but practice varies with the speaker and both are correct.

For a regular action, mainly in Portugal:

Eu tenho aulas de Português <u>à</u> quarta e sexta. /
Eu tenho aulas de Português <u>às</u> quartas e sextas.
I have Portuguese classes on Wednesday(s) and Friday(s).

For a regular action, mainly in Brazil:

Eu tenho aulas de Português <u>nas</u> quartas e sextas.
I have Portuguese classes on Wednesdays and Fridays.

Where **em** is used for a single action, an expression of time for past and future can be used but it is not always necessary.

Eu fui ao cinema <u>na</u>   *I went to the cinema last Friday.*
   <u>passada sexta</u>.
Eu fui ao cinema   *I went to the cinema on Friday.*
   <u>na sexta</u>.   (it is understood it was last Friday)
Eu vou ao cinema <u>na</u>   *I am going to the cinema next Friday.*
   <u>próxima sexta</u>.
Eu vou ao cinema <u>na</u>   *I am going to the cinema on Friday.*
   <u>sexta</u>.   (it is understood it will be next
    Friday)

41 Esse ou aquele? *That one or that one?* (This, that ... and that)

In English, we use *this* and *that* to determine or point to the noun we mean. In Portuguese, though, there are three words (demonstrative pronouns):

isto	*this* (near you)
isso	*that* (near the person/people you are addressing)
aquilo	*that over there* (away from both of you)

Despite their masculine ending, these words are in fact neuter, and don't change for gender or number – they mean *this thing* or *that thing*:

O que é isso?	*What is that (in your hand)?*
Isto é uma caneta.	*This is a pen.*

These demonstrative pronouns won't do when you want to say, for example *this book*, or *that car*. Instead we need to use demonstrative adjectives. Again there are three, but this time they do agree with the number and gender of the noun they are associated with:

Masculine	Feminine	
este(s)	**esta(s)**	*this* (near you)
esse (s)	**essa(s)**	*that* (near the person/people you are addressing)
aquele(s)	**aquela(s)**	*that* (away from both of you)

You can use these masculine/feminine/singular/plural forms as demonstrative pronouns if you know the object they refer to – and know its gender and number. You can see this in the example set in a garden below, when the mother says to her daughter: **essa é uma orquídea** and **rosas são aquelas**.

> **Daughter:** Mamã*, <u>esta</u> flor é uma rosa?
> *Mummy, is this flower (near me) a rose?*
>
> **Mother:** Não, minha querida, <u>essa</u> é uma orquídea. Rosas são <u>aquelas</u> junto do lago.
> *No, darling, that one is an orchid. Roses are those (over there) by the lake.*

*A Brazilian child would say **Mamãe**

When **de** contracts with these demonstratives, they will then start with 'd-' – **disto, deste, desta**, etc. When **em** contracts with them, we have **nisto, neste, nesta**, etc.

> **Daughter:** Gosto mais <u>daquelas</u>. São muito bonitas.
> *I like those better. They are very pretty.* (meaning the roses) **Mamã, e o que é <u>aquilo</u> no lago? Também é uma flor?** *Mummy, and what is that thing in the lake? Is it also a flower?*
>
> **Mother:** É sim. <u>Aquela</u> flor é um nenúfar.
> *Yes, it is. That flower is a water-lily.*

Please note that the distinction between demonstratives **isto, isso** and **aquilo** (and **este, esse, aquele,** etc.) runs parallel to the distinction between adverbs **aqui,** *here,* **aí,** *there,* and **ali,** *over there* (see Chapter 42).

42a O livro está aí ou ali? *Is the book by you or over there?* (Here, there … and there)

HERE **AND** *THERE*

You mustn't forget that for *here* and *there* you have a further distinction to make in Portuguese.

aqui	*here* (near you)
aí	*there* (near the person/people you are addressing)
ali	*over there* (away from both you and the person/people you are addressing)

<u>Aqui</u> em Lisboa nunca neva.	*Here in Lisbon it never snows.*
Acho que o livro está <u>aí</u> na gaveta ao seu lado.	*I think the book is there by you inside the drawer.*
Venham ver a minha casa. <u>Aqui</u> é a sala e <u>ali</u> o quarto.	*Come and have a tour of my place. Here we have the living room and over there the bedroom.*
Diz <u>aqui</u> no jornal que vai haver greve dos motoristas de táxi.	*It says here in the newspaper that taxi drivers are going to go on strike.*

CONTRACTED FORMS

When **de** contracts with **aqui**, **aí** and **ali**, the resulting forms are **daqui**, **daí** and **dali**.

EXAMPLES

On the telephone:

Ana:	A que horas partem <u>daí</u>?
	What time are you leaving (from there, where you are)?
José:	Partimos <u>daqui</u> às 10 horas.
	We are leaving (from here) at 10 o'clock.

98

In a lecture:

Augusto: Venha para <u>aqui</u>, <u>daí</u> não vê bem.
Come over here, you can't see properly from there.

Rosa: Esse lugar <u>aí</u> não está ocupado? Então mudo.
<u>Daqui</u> não vejo nada.
Is that seat (there) by you not taken? Then I'll move over. I can't see anything from here.

After changing seats,

Rosa: <u>Dali</u> também não ouvia bem.
I couldn't hear properly from there (where I was) either.

42b Cá chove menos do que lá *Around here it rains less than there* (Here, there... and there)

In 42a we looked at the distinction between **aqui** – *here*, **aí** – *there* (near the person / people you are addressing) – and **ali** – *over there* (away from both you and the person / people you are addressing). Now we can move on to something else.

There is a further distinction to consider, **cá** and **lá**. Although their meaning is basically the same as **aqui** and **ali**, they are not always interchangeable. Generally **cá** and **lá** are for less specific locations or when the place is not explicitly mentioned.

<u>Cá</u> em Portugal bebe-se mais café do que chá.	*Here in Portugal we drink more coffee than tea.* (all over Portugal, no specific region)
Gosto muito de Paris. Fui <u>lá</u> a semana passada.	*I like Paris very much. I went there last week.* (Paris in general)

However, **cá** and **lá** are very frequently used in colloquial speech when giving or receiving something:

Tome <u>lá</u>.	*There you are.* (literally, *Take it*)
Dê <u>cá</u>.	*Give it to me.* (literally, *Give it here*)

....

SPACE AND LOCATION → TIME

The adverbs above (**aqui, aí, cá,** etc.) are to do with space and location, but they can also be applied to time.

Estará tudo pronto <u>daqui</u> a cinco minutos.	*Everything will be ready in five minutes.*
O avião parte <u>daqui</u> a uma hora.	*The aeroplane is leaving one hour from now.*
Tenciono visitar Moçambique <u>daqui</u> a um ano.	*I intend to visit Mozambique in one year's time.*
Ele chegou <u>dali</u> a pouco.	*He arrived shortly afterwards.*

Don't forget that the distinction between **aqui (cá), aí, ali (lá)** runs parallel to the distinction between the demonstratives (see chapter 41) and they are often used together:

Costumava ser assim <u>lá naquela</u>   *That's how it used to be in the*
   época.   *(those) old days.*
<u>Isto aqui</u> é o meu novo   *This (here) is my new laptop.*
   computador portátil.
Desculpe, <u>essa</u> cadeira <u>aí</u>   *Excuse me, is that chair*
   está livre?   *(by you) free?*
<u>Aquele</u> rapaz <u>ali</u> é o meu filho.   *That boy (over there) is my son.*

43 Ele é o melhor aluno *He is the best student* (Degrees of comparison)

The comparative and superlative forms of **grande, bom** and **mau** often catch people out! They bear no resemblance to the original adjective. While in most instances, you say something is *more ... than* (*more beautiful than*, for instance) by placing the adjective between **mais** and **do que** (**mais bonito do que**), you cannot do that to **grande, bom** and **mau**.

Note that in **do que, do** is optional and often not heard in the spoken language. Let's now look at this in detail in the table below.

Adjective	Comparative	Superlative
alto/a	**mais alto/a (do) que**	**o/a mais alto/a**
tall	*taller than*	*the tallest*
grande	**maior (do) que**	**o/a maior**
big, large	*bigger, larger than*	*the biggest, largest*
bom / boa	**melhor (do) que**	**o/a melhor**
good	*better than*	*the best*
mau / má *	**pior (do) que**	**o/a pior**
bad	*worse than*	*the worst*

*In Brazil **ruim** is often preferred for *bad* and **mau/má** reserved for connotations of *evil, wicked*.

In the same way that **altíssimo/a** (*very tall*) is an alternative to **muito alto/a, ótimo / ótima** is the same as **muito bom / boa** (*very good*) and **péssimo / péssima** the same as **muito mau / má** (*very bad*). **Enorme** (*huge, enormous*) is often used instead of **muito grande** (*very big, large*).

Francisco:	**Tive boas notas. Fui <u>o melhor</u> aluno da turma.**
	My marks were good. I was the best student in the class.
Roberto:	**Parabéns! Eu acho que fui <u>o pior</u>...**
	Congratulations! I think I was the worst ...

Onde vamos? A comida do restaurante O Coelho <u>é melhor</u> do que a do Pescador mas também é mais cara.
Where shall we go? The food at the O Coelho restaurant is better than that of the Pescador but it is also more expensive.

Os planos para a nova sede da empresa mostram que vai ser um edifício <u>enorme</u>. Isso é <u>ótimo</u> porque temos crescido muito.
The plans for the new company headquarters show it is going to be a huge building. That's great because we have grown a lot.

Na exposição de vegetais havia abóboras muito grandes. <u>A maior</u> pesava 20 kg.
At the vegetable show there were very large pumpkins. The biggest weighed 20 kg.

The comparative and superlative of the adverbs **bem** (*well*) and **mal** (*badly*) are identical to those of **bom** and **mau**:

Hoje ainda estou adoentado, mas ontem estava muito <u>pior</u>.	*I'm still unwell today, but yesterday I was much worse.*

OTHERS

▶ menor = mais pequeno (*smaller/smallest*)

Menor is preferred in Brazil, **mais pequeno** in Portugal.

O cachorrinho <u>mais pequeno</u> (Portugal) / <u>menor</u> (Brazil) é o Pipocas.
Pipocas is the smallest puppy.

▶ máximo, mínimo (*maximum, minimum*)
▶ superior, inferior (*superior, inferior*)

Se há um salário <u>mínimo</u>, que tal também um salário <u>máximo</u>?	*If there is a minimum salary, what about a maximum?*
A qualidade deste tecido é <u>superior</u> à desse.	*This fabric is better quality than that one.*

44 Seis pãezinhos, por favor *Six bread rolls, please* (Augmentatives and diminutives)

Don't forget the suffixes, those small additions to the ends of words that give them additional meanings. Portuguese makes good use of suffixes. At the top of the list, please bear in mind -ão and -inho for opposite effects. You will need them for some notions English expresses in quite a different way.

▶ -ão is an augmentative. It exaggerates the features conveyed by the original word.

Literal:

(a) garrafa *bottle*   **(o) garrafão** *demijohn*
(a) porta *door*   **(o) portão** *gate*
(o) papel *paper*   **(o) papelão** *cardboard*

Less literal:

(o) rapaz *boy, lad*   **(o) rapagão** *big boy* (not just in size)
(a) palavra *word*   **(o) palavrão** *swear word*

▶ -inho is a diminutive which attributes the notion of smallness and affection.

Literal:

(o) pão *loaf of bread*   **(o) pãozinho** *bread roll*
(o) café *coffee*   **(o) cafezinho** *small cup of coffee*

Please note the plural of **pãozinho**:

(os) pãezinhos, from **pães + inhos**

Less literal level, adding some overtones (*cute*, etc.):

(a) casa *house*	**(a) casinha** *little house*
(o) rapaz *boy, lad*	**(o) rapazinho** *little boy* (but growing up)

Expressing affection:

(a) mãe *mother*	**(a) mãezinha** *mummy*
(o) pai *father*	**(o) paizinho** *daddy*

▶ **-ria** or **-aria** is another useful suffix, used for names of shops:

(o) pão *bread, loaf*	**(a) padaria** *baker's shop, bakery*
(o) papel *paper*	**(a) papelaria** *stationery shop*
(o) sapato *shoe*	**(a) sapataria** *shoe shop*
(o) livro *book*	**(a) livraria** *bookshop, bookstore*

45 Por favor *Please* (Polite requests)

In English you would sound rather rude if you didn't say *please* when you ask for something – *come here!*, *give me that!* – and *thank you* afterwards.

In Portuguese, the verb forms you use to make a request have an inbuilt element of politeness. So, please say **por favor** to start with but there is no need to keep repeating the phrase. As for **obrigado / obrigada** (*thank you* said by male/female), say it just once at the end.

When you say for instance **dê** (*give*) from **dar** (*to give*) or **traga** (*bring*) from **trazer** (*to bring*), you are using the present subjunctive of the verb, which is used to express wishes, hypothetical situations and uncertainty and therefore politeness.

When talking to friends or children, most people are more likely to say **dá** (*give*) or **traz** (*bring*). This is the second person imperative, to show a more familiar approach.

When you express your request by saying **(eu) queria** (the imperfect of **querer**) – *I would like* – you are using another type of polite verb form. The imperfect is also very often used in questions for polite requests.

Queria uma garrafa de vinho.	*I would like a bottle of wine.*
Trazia uma garrafa de vinho?	*Could/would you bring a bottle of wine?*
Trazia mais um copo?	*Could/would you bring another glass?*
Podia me dizer as horas?	*Could/would you tell me the time?*

And yet again you are being polite when, for instance, in a shop you say simply **por favor** before placing your request.

Study the following exchange between a female customer and a shop assistant at the delicatessen counter of a supermarket.

Customer	Por favor, meio quilo de queijo.	*1/2 kg cheese, please.*
Shop assistant	Mais alguma coisa?	*Anything else?*
Customer	Dê-me(*) meia dúzia de salsichas.	*Give me half a dozen sausages.*
Shop assistant	Mais alguma coisa?	*Anything else?*
Customer	Queria 250 g de salada.	*I would like 250 g of salad.*
Shop assistant	Mais alguma coisa?	*Anything else?*
Customer	Não, mais nada. <u>Obrigada</u>.	*Nothing else. Thank you.*

(*) In Brazil you are likely to hear **Me dê ...**

Now study the following exchange between a male customer and a café waiter.

Customer	Por favor, traga uma água mineral.	*Please bring (me) a mineral water.*
Waiter	E para comer?	*Anything to eat?*
Customer	Queria um pastel de nata.	*I would like a custard tart.*
Waiter	Mais alguma coisa?	*Anything else?*
Customer	Não, é tudo. Obrigado.	*No, that's all. Thank you.*

So, in this sort of situation, you should use **por favor** or another polite expression, but there is no need to overdo it. The same applies to **obrigado / obrigada**.

Insight

Some other useful polite requests:

Abra / feche a janela / porta.	*Open/close the window/door.*
Pague na caixa.	*Pay at the till.*
Desligue o telefone / computador.	*Turn off the phone/computer.*
Acenda / apague a luz.	*Switch on/off the light.*
Esteja no café às 3h.	*Be in the café at 3 o'clock.*

46 O senhor, você ou tu? *You, you or you?* (Forms of address)

There are three ways of saying *you* in Portuguese and this section will help you make the right choice.

HOW ARE YOU?

Look at the following three different ways of saying *How are you?*

O senhor, <u>como vai</u>?	polite (and formal) – to a man
A senhora, <u>como vai</u>?	polite (and formal) – to a woman
Você, <u>como vai</u>?	general
<u>Como vais</u>?	for close relations, friends and children

O/a senhor(a) and você share the same verb form – vai. If you say simply como vai?, your approach will be very neutral.

Vais shows that you are addressing close relations, friends and children. You don't need to use an equivalent to o/a senhor(a) or você, but if you do, use tu.

COURTESY TITLES (MR, MRS, ETC.)

With or without an initial capital Senhora corresponds to *Ms/Mrs/Miss*. Senhor corresponds to *Mr*.

There appears to be a lot of misunderstanding in respect of some titles. This stems mainly from two combined factors, the use of *Dr* in English and the Portuguese language practice of titling people by their professional activity.

In English, the title *Dr* is mainly associated with the word *doctor* as a common noun for a qualified practitioner of medicine, regardless of whether s/he holds a doctorate degree. In Portuguese, the title **Dr / Dr^a** is mainly associated with academic qualifications. The common word for *doctor* is **médico** or **médica** (male or female). A distinction can be made between **Doutor(a)**, for someone with a doctorate, and **doutor(a)** for a holder of a lower degree. The latter – **senhor(a) doutor(a)** – is equivalent in status to, for instance, **senhor(a) engenheiro/a** *(engineer)*, **senhor(a) arquiteto/a** *(architect)*, etc., that is, a professional rather than academic title. **Senhor** and **senhora** are widely used. As regards professional titles, nowadays they tend to be used more sparingly.

TERMS OF ADDRESS

Although **senhor / senhora** can be translated as *sir/madam*, they are not as ceremonious as the translation may suggest. In Portuguese people often address each other as **o senhor / a senhora** as a matter of courtesy.

O senhor fala Português?	*Do you speak Portuguese?*

Você is the general approach, with or without the word **você**.

Eu falo Português. E você também?	*I speak Portuguese. Do you too?*
(Você) fala Português?	*Do you speak Portuguese?*

Tu is used for close relations, friends and children. It is is used among fellow students to show comradeship.

Eu falo Português. E tu também?	*I speak Portuguese. Do you too?*

In most of Brazil, however, **tu** is not used much as such, but the pronoun **te** is sometimes used in combination with **você**.

Você estava no hotel? Não te vi lá.	*Were you in the hotel? I didn't see you there.*

The subtleties between **tu** and **você** disappear when you address more than one person, for **vocês** is the plural of both.

Vocês querem tomar alguma coisa?	*Would you (more than one) like a drink?*
Vocês querem vir comigo para a praia?	*Would you (more than one) like to come to the beach with me?*
(Eu) comprei isto para vocês.	*I have bought this for you (more than one).*

47 Filhos e crianças *Children and children*
('Child', 'son' and 'daughter')

Portuguese uses the word **criança** for children in general but when you are asking someone about their children in the sense of *son* or *daughter* you use **filho** and **filha.**

AS CRIANÇAS (*CHILDREN*)

If you are looking for facilities for children, you would say:

O hotel tem piscina para   *Does this hotel have a pool for*
  crianças?   *young children?*

If you are buying tickets, you would say:

Quatro, por favor, para dois adultos e duas <u>crianças</u>.

or more briefly,

Quatro, por favor, dois adultos e duas <u>crianças</u>.
Four, please, two adults and two <u>children</u>.

Note that the word **a criança** is always feminine whether referring to a male or a female child.

Aquela criança é o meu filho.	*That child is my son.*
Aquela criança é a minha filha.	*That child is my daughter.*
O seu neto é uma criança muito bonita.	*Your grandson is a very pretty child.*

OS FILHOS (*CHILDREN*)

Here are some useful phrases when talking about your own children:

One child:

Tenho um filho.	*I have a son.*
Ele é filho único.	*He is an only child.*
Tenho uma filha.	*I have a daughter.*
Ela é filha única.	*She is an only child.*

More than one child:

Tenho dois filhos.	*I have two sons.*
Tenho duas filhas.	*I have two daughters.*
Tenho dois filhos.	*I have two children (male and female).*
Tenho três filhos.	*I have three sons.*
Tenho três filhos.	*I have three children (male and female).*
Tenho uma filha e um filho, ambos casados.	*I have a daughter and a son, both married.*
Tenho uma filha casada e um filho solteiro.	*I have a married daughter and an unmarried son.*

Insight

When referring to someone's children or your own, don't say **as crianças** if they are grown up.

If you say **uma criança única**, that will not mean *an only child* but *a unique child*!

48 A gente desta terra *The people of this land* (Nouns which function in both the singular and plural)

In English, there are some nouns (*crew, police, government, family*) which can function as singular or plural. This is not the case in Portuguese. *The crew were very kind* is in Portuguese **A tripulação foi muito simpática.** Other examples are:

A polícia chegou rapidamente quando fui atacada.
The police arrived quickly when I was attacked.

Estava uma grande multidão no aeroporto porque chegava um cantor famoso.
There was a big crowd at the airport because a famous singer was arriving.

If individuals are thought of, then that must be specified.

Os membros da tripulação foram muito simpáticos.
The crew (the crew members) were very kind.

Quatro elementos da polícia chegaram rapidamente quando fui atacada.
Four police officers arrived quickly when I was attacked.

Other Portuguese nouns denoting groups:

(o) exército *army*
(a) marinha *navy, fleet*
(a) armada *navy*
(o) povo *people* (in the sense of *inhabitants of a country*)

O povo português é simpático.   *Portuguese people are nice.*

As well as meaning *nation*, etc., the English word *people* is also, and perhaps primarily, the plural of *person*. In this sense, you will need Portuguese **(as) pessoas**, plural of **(a) pessoa.**

As pessoas que <u>moram</u> ao meu lado são simpáticas. *The people who <u>live</u> next to me are nice.*

THE PORTUGUESE WORD 'GENTE'

▶ As a noun similar to *crew*, *people*, etc.

<u>a gente</u> desta terra   *the people of this land*

▶ To denote the size of a crowd

muita gente   *several/many people*
pouca gente   *few people*

Hoje é feriado e está calor. <u>Está</u> muita gente na praia.
Today it is a holiday and it is hot. <u>There are</u> many people on the beach.

O filme tem atores muito conhecidos mas hoje <u>está</u> pouca gente no cinema.
The film has well known actors but today <u>there are</u> few people in the cinema.

▶ As a pronoun standing for *people* or *I* or any person like me:

A gente nunca <u>usa</u> essa palavra.
One never <u>says</u> that word./We never <u>say</u> that word.

▶ In colloquial speech, as an alternative to the personal pronoun nós:

A gente <u>vai</u> à praia. Queres vir também?

is the same as:

Nós <u>vamos</u> à praia. Queres vir também?   *We <u>are</u> going to the beach. Do you want to come too?*

49a Saber – conhecer, conseguir – poder *To know, to be able to, can* (Discerning verb meanings)

There are some pairs of verbs that confuse learners mainly when their different meanings have only one translation in English. There are distinctions you need to make.

'SABER' – 'CONHECER' *TO KNOW*

▶ Saber is *to know facts or things, to be able to, to understand,* and therefore is used for skills or general knowledge.

Sabemos falar francês.	*We can (know how to) speak French.*
Ela sabe tocar piano muito bem.	*She can play the piano very well.*
Sabem o que foi discutido na reunião?	*Do you know what was discussed in the meeting?*

Remember that the form for **eu** in the present is **sei**:

Sei que o João comprou uma casa.	*I know that João has bought a house.*

▶ Conhecer means *to be acquainted with,* therefore it is used for people and places.

Conheço o Ricardo; foi meu colega na escola.	*I know Ricardo; he went to school with me.*
Eles conhecem Luanda muito bem porque viveram lá 5 anos.	*They know Luanda very well because they lived there for 5 years.*

▶ Notice the difference:

Sabemos onde é Moscovo, mas não conhecemos Moscovo.	*We know where Moscow is, but we don't know Moscow.*

'PODER' – 'CONSEGUIR' *TO BE ABLE, CAN*

▶ While **conseguir** implies a degree of effort, **poder** doesn't.

Ela não pode ir ao cinema porque tem de estudar.	*She can't go to the cinema because she needs to study.*
Acabei o trabalho de casa: agora posso ir às compras	*I've finished my homework: now I can go shopping.*
Conseguiu fazer as palavras cruzadas em 10 minutos!!!	*You were able to do the crossword in 10 minutes!!!*
Ela não consegue resolver este problema – é muito difícil.	*She can't solve this problem – it's very difficult.*
Não consegui lembrar-me de tudo o que tinha para dizer.	*I couldn't remember everything I had to say.*

▶ **Poder** can also mean *may, to be allowed.*

Posso entrar?	*May I come in?*
Não podem tomar banho quando a bandeira está vermelha.	*You can't (aren't allowed to) bathe when the flag is red.*
Claro que não se pode fumar no cinema. É proibido.	*Of course one can't smoke in the cinema. It's forbidden.*

49b Pedir – perguntar, dever – ter de *Asking and obligation* (Discerning verb meanings)

In 49a we looked at a number of tricky semantic distinctions between some verbs. There are further examples to consider.

'PEDIR' – 'PERGUNTAR' *TO ASK*

▶ **Pedir** is *to request.*

Não conheço esta zona. Vou ao Turismo pedir informações.	*I don't know this area. I'm going to the Tourist Office to request information.*
Ela pediu para sair mais cedo.	*She asked to leave earlier.*

▶ **Perguntar** means *to enquire.*

O professor pergunta sempre se fizemos o trabalho de casa.	*The teacher always asks us whether we've done our homework.*
Perguntei a um polícia o caminho para a praia.	*I asked a policeman the way to the beach.*

► *To ask a question* is translated by **fazer** uma pergunta.

Vou fazer essa pergunta na próxima reunião.   *I am going to ask that question at the next meeting.*

► Perguntar <u>por</u> is *to ask about/for.*

Encontrei hoje o Júlio; perguntou por si.   *I met Júlio today; he asked about you.*

Perguntei pelo livro à Inês mas ela não o tinha trazido.   *I asked Inês for the book but she hadn't brought it.*

'TER DE/QUE' – 'DEVER' *MUST*

► Ter de/que implies obligation, *to have to* do something.

Tenho de meter gasolina no carro.   *I must put petrol in the car.*

Vocês têm que comprar os bilhetes na estação.   *You have to buy the tickets at the station.*

► Dever suggests a possibility or probability.

A reunião deve ser no dia do costume.   *The meeting must (is likely to) be on the usual day.*

Dever can also convey a moral obligation or mean *to owe.*

Devemos tratar bem os animais.   *We must (ought to) treat animals well.*

Não deve estacionar em frente da porta porque dificulta a saída dos moradores.   *You mustn't (shouldn't) park in front of the door because it makes it difficult for the residents to get out.*

Comprei o livro que me pediste. Deves-me €15.20.   *I bought the book you asked. You owe me €15.20.*

50a Puxe, pilha, geleia de laranja e um lanche *Pull, battery, marmalade and a snack* (False friends)

You may be misled by the meaning of an English word when you hear or see a Portuguese word that sounds or looks similar but in fact has a different meaning. This may result in amusement but can also lead to embarrassment. In this last chapter we are going to look at how to avoid a number of such pitfalls in the course of everyday life.

'PUXE PARA ABRIR' – *PULL TO OPEN*

Portuguese **puxe** sounds very much like English *push* but means *pull*. If someone says **Puxe!** as you are trying to open a door, remember that means *Pull!*

The word **puxe** is the present subjunctive of the verb **puxar**, *to pull*, to express a request asking someone to do something – *pull!*

If you see **puxe** or **puxar** on a door you should pull it to open, and if you see **empurre** or **empurrar**, you should push.

'BATERIAS E PILHAS' – *BATTERIES AND BATTERIES*

If you need batteries for your torch or camera, ask for **pilhas** – **a pilha**.

Bateria – **a bateria** – is a car battery or it can mean drums in the percussion section of an orchestra or rock band.

MARMALADE – 'GELEIA DE LARANJA'

You may like marmalade on your toast at breakfast. What you need is **a geleia de laranja**.

Although *marmalade* is originally a Portuguese word – **a marmelada** – its original meaning has been changed since its adoption by English. *Marmalade* and **marmelada** are different types of fruit preserve.

The original **marmelada** is a fruit paste made from **o marmelo**, *quince*. Paste can also be made from other fruits: **marmelada de maçã, marmelada de goiaba**, etc. For marmalade as you probably know it, ask for **a geleia de laranja** or **o doce de laranja**.

LANCHES E ALMOÇOS – *SNACKS AND LUNCHES*

When you are invited to lunch, the word you will hear is **almoço** – **o almoço**, *lunch*, or **almoçar**, *to have lunch*. The Portuguese word **lanche** – **o lanche** – means a *snack*, something light you eat between main meals; **lanchar** means *to have a snack*.

50b Pais, comum, bonito e um copo *Parents, ordinary, exquisite and a glass* (More false friends)

In 50a we looked at some misleading similarities between English and Portuguese words. We are now going to look at false friends that can interfere when you are trying to socialize. Be the winner and celebrate your good command of Portuguese with a toast!

'PARENTES E PAIS' – *RELATIONS AND PARENTS*

If what you mean is *parents*, say **os pais**. You can also say **pai** – **o pai** – *father*, and **mãe** – **a mãe** – *mother*, for, respectively, a male and female parent. You would use the word **parentes** when talking about your relations in general.

Os meus pais tinham uma quinta no Minho.	*My parents had an estate in the Minho region.*
Os meus parentes moram em Lisboa.	*My family lives in Lisbon.*

'ORDINÁRIO E COMUM' – *COMMON AND ORDINARY*

The Portuguese word **ordinário** means *vulgar*, *common*. On the other hand, **comum** does not have pejorative overtones. It's better not to describe yourself or anyone else as **ordinário/a** because you won't make many friends!

'ESQUISITO...' – *WEIRD...*

Esquisito is another word which should be used with care. This does not mean *exquisite*, but *funny*, in the sense of strange, odd, weird. Your blunder may have undesirable social consequences.

If you wish to compliment someone on what they are wearing, you could say, for instance:

Que vestido tão bonito!	*What a pretty dress!*
Que chapéu tão bonito!	*What a pretty hat!*

Que blusa tão bonita!
Que sapatos tão bonitos!

What a pretty blouse!
Your shoes are very pretty!

'COPOS E CANECAS' – *GLASSES AND MUGS*

You may think that **copo** means *cup*, but this isn't so.

Portuguese (o) **copo** translates English *glass* and *tumbler*. It is a drinking vessel made out of glass, plastic or other material, which doesn't have a handle.

For a drinking vessel with a handle, use (a) **caneca** for *mug*. For a smaller, more delicate cup you can say (a) **xícara**, and in Portugal preferably (a) **chávena**.

Glossary of grammatical terms

a/o – see **o/a**

accents (graphic) – written marks above letters that are placed above a vowel in Portuguese to indicate its quality or stress, like in **chá**, *tea*, **à**, *to the*, **você**, *you*.

acute (accent) – right-to-left oblique mark above a vowel showing á stressed open sound, like in **chá**, *tea*.

adjective – a word that adds information about a noun by describing or qualifying it – **o carro é <u>novo</u>**, *the car is <u>new</u>*.

adjective-like – words like past participles and ordinals when they are giving information about a noun – **a porta está <u>fechada</u>**, *the door is <u>closed</u>*, **a <u>primeira</u> rua depois do semáforo**, *the <u>first</u> road after the traffic lights*.

adverb – a word that gives information about a verb – **nós estamos <u>bem</u>**, *we are <u>well</u>*, **nós fomos <u>lá</u>**, *we went <u>there</u>*; and some adverbs can also give information about an adjective – **este carro é <u>muito</u> caro**, *this car is <u>very</u> expensive*.

agreement – this is when two or more words have to take on matching grammatical features, as is the case with gender and number endings in Portuguese nouns and associated words – **<u>os</u> carr<u>os</u> nov<u>os</u>**, *the new cars*.

apposition – a word or phrase is said to be in apposition to another when it is placed immediately after it, usually between commas, in order to give additional information to the original word or phrase – **Maria, <u>a nossa filha</u>, está no hotel**, *Maria, <u>our daughter</u>, is at the hotel*.

article – see **definite article** and **indefinite article**.

augmentative – a type of suffix that attributes exaggerated features to the original word – **papel**, *paper* → **papelão**, *cardboard (thick paper)*.

cardinals or cardinal numbers – *one, two, three, etc.* (**um/uma, dois/duas, três, etc.**)

cedilha – the Portuguese name for a mark written under letter **c** which in Portuguese shows that this letter represents a soft sound like in **preço**, *price*, as opposed to a hard sound like in **carro**, *car*.

circumflex (accent) – two joined-up oblique lines above a vowel showing a close (closed) sound, like in **você**, *you*.

close (vowel) – pronounced with a relatively narrow opening of the mouth, like in English *note* or in Portuguese **novo**, *new*.

command – these are requests and orders and can be expressed in Portuguese by the imperative or the present subjunctive – **Entre!**, *Come in!*, **Não entre!**, *Don't come in!* (verb **entrar**, *to enter*).

comparatives – forms of adjectives and adverbs used to make comparisons – **mais interessante**, *more interesting*, **mais depressa**, *more quickly*.

conditional – this expresses English *I should/would (do/be)* – **eu gostaria de ficar aqui um mês**, *I should/would like to stay here for a month*.

conjugate – that is when you give different endings and forms to a verb – **eu telefono**, *I phone*, **ele telefona**, *he phones*, **eles telefonaram**, *they phoned*.

consonant – a speech sound in which the breath is partially obstructed, as in b, c, d, etc. – a c̲a̲deir̲a, *chair*.

contractions – these are a fusion of two words – em, *in/on* + o, *the* = no, *in/on the*; de, *from* + aqui, *here* = daqui, *from here*.

definite article – like English *the*, the Portuguese definite article precedes a noun which is presented as a specific item but will be either masculine or feminine – o̲ carro (masculine), *car*, a̲ casa (feminine), *house*.

demonstrative – a word that determines which noun you mean (more precisely than *the*) and may stand for a noun as well as a pronoun, e.g. este carro é novo, *this car is new*, isto é novo, *this (thing) is new*.

diacritic – mark used to indicate different sounds or values of a letter – c → ç, o → ó.

digraph – a group of two letters representing one phoneme, or speech sound, as English 'ph' in p̲h̲armacy or Portuguese 'nh' in a senhora, *lady*, 'rr' in o carro, *car*, and 'im' in sim.

diminutive – a type of suffix that attributes the notions of smallness and affection to the original word – rapaz, *boy* → rapazinho, *little boy*.

diphthong – where articulation begins as one vowel and moves to another, as in English *loud* or Portuguese pa̲i̲, *father* (oral diphthong), and mãe̲, *mother* (nasal diphthong).

false friends – words that look or sound the same in two languages but have different meanings like English *cup* and Portuguese o copo, *glass* or *tumbler*, not a *cup*.

feminine – see **gender**.

forms of address – the Portuguese main forms of address are, for a formal approach, **o senhor / a senhora**, *sir/madam*, for a less formal, more general approach, **você**, *you*, and for a more familiar approach **tu**, *you* (in Brazil mainly as personal pronoun object **te**).

future – see **tense**.

gender – nouns, adjectives, adjective-like words and pronouns have what is called grammatical gender even if they don't refer to anything which is clearly male or female – **o carro**, *the car*, is masculine in Portuguese; and there are also neuter words – **isto**, *this (thing)* (the Portuguese word has a masculine ending, '-o', but acts as a neuter).

grammar – the rules of standard language practice.

grave (accent) – left-to-right oblique mark above a vowel showing an open sound, e.g. **à**, *to the*.

imperative – see **command**.

imperfect – a past tense which denotes an action or state over a period of time in the past – **nesse tempo eu ia à praia todas as semanas**, *in those days I used to go to the beach every week*.

indefinite article –English *a/an*; in Portuguese the indefinite article precedes a noun which denotes something general, not particular – <u>um</u> **carro** (masculine), *car*, <u>uma</u> **casa** (feminine), *house*.

indicative – see **mood**.

infinitive – the basic form of a verb (how it usually appears in a dictionary). In English it consists of two parts, e.g. *to burn* but Portuguese verbs have distinctive endings: **-ar, -er, -ir** or **-or**: **comprar**, *to buy*, **vender**, *to sell*, **partir**, *to leave*, **supor**, *to suppose*.

inflections – changes to a word to express tense, mood, person, gender, number, etc.

inflected infinitive – see **personal infinitive**.

Latin – the ancient language from which Portuguese derives, as well as Catalan, French, Italian, Romanian and Spanish.

masculine – see **gender**.

mode of address – the way you relate to others in face-to-face speech, or in writing, and the way media organizations address their audience or readership. (see also **forms of address**)

mood – the different sets of verb changes used to denote facts (indicative mood) or a probability (subjunctive mood) – **ela veio** ontem, *she came yesterday* (indicative), **eu espero que ele venha** amanhã, *I hope he may come tomorrow* (subjunctive).

nasal sound – when the air stream passes through the nose as a result of the lowering of the soft palate at the back of the mouth, like in English ending '-ing' – **singing** – and in the Portuguese words **sim**, *yes*, and **não**, *no*.

neuter – see **gender**.

noun – a naming word for a person, animal, place, thing, or idea – o **homem**, *man*, (a) **Maria**, *Mary*, a **praia**, *beach*, o **carro**, *car*, o **pensamento**, *thought*. Nouns in Portuguese are either masculine or feminine.

number – whether just one is meant (singular) or more than one (plural), as in o **carro novo**, *the new car*, **ele mora aqui**, *he lives here*, as opposed to **os carros novos**, *the new cars*, **eles moram aqui**, *they live here*.

numerals – numbers (see also **cardinals** and **ordinals**).

o/a – it can be the definite article or a pronoun – <u>a</u> mala do David e <u>a</u> da Rita, *David's suitcase and Rita's*, literally, *the suitcase of David and the one of Rita* – (definite article in <u>a</u> mala do..., pronoun in <u>a</u> da...).

open (vowel) – pronounced with a relatively wide opening of the mouth, like in English 'ah' or in Portuguese m<u>a</u>pa, *map*.

ordinals or **ordinal numbers** – *first, second, third*, etc. (primeiro/a, segundo/a, terceiro/a)

orthography – spelling rules.

past – see **tense**.

past participle – a verb form that shows the end result of an action, as in o vidro <u>quebrado</u>, *the <u>broken</u> glass*, a porta <u>fechada</u>, *the <u>closed</u> door*.

person – the subject of an action or state of being.

personal infinitive – the infinitive of Portuguese verbs can take personal endings, so as to provide information about the doer of an action – ao abrir<u>mos</u> a porta, *on us opening the door/ when we opened the door*.

personal object pronoun – *me, you, him, her*, etc. (me, te, lhe, etc.)

personal subject pronoun – *I, you, he, she*, etc. (eu, tu, você, ele, ela, etc.)

phoneme – a speech sound; in some cases it can be used to distinguish one word from another, as in a <u>s</u>esta, *afternoon nap*, and a <u>f</u>esta, *party*.

phonetics – the sounds of a language.

plural – see **number**.

possessives – words that show ownership or belonging and can be either adjectives – **a minha mala**, *my suitcase* – or pronouns – **a minha**, *mine*.

prepositions – words that show the relationship of one thing to another – **de**, *of*, *from*, **em**, *in*, *on*, **por**, *by*, *for*.

present – see tense.

preterite – a past tense that presents an action or state as a whole that happened at a point in time – **ontem fui à praia**, *yesterday I went to the beach*.

pronoun – a word that stands in place of a noun, as in **ela**, *she*, when talking about Mary, or **isto**, *this (thing)*, without saying what it is.

proper noun – a name (noun) used for an individual person, place, country, etc. – **Maria, Copacabana, Portugal**.

reflexive pronouns – *myself, yourself, him/herself*, etc. (**me, te, se**, etc.) – **o menino não <u>se</u> lavou bem**, *the little boy didn't wash <u>himself</u> properly*.

reflexive verbs – verbs for an action that reflects back on the subject carrying out the action – **eles divertiram-se**, *they enjoyed themselves*.

semantic – to do with both the basic meaning and connotations of words and sentences.

silent – said of a letter that is not pronounced, like English 'b' in *dou<u>b</u>t* and Portuguese 'h' at the beginning of word, as in **o <u>h</u>omem**, *man*.

singular – see **number**.

stressed syllable – the word segment that is pronounced more forcefully – a m<u>e</u>sa, *table*, a bat<u>a</u>ta, *potato*.

subject – the doer of an action or the bearer of a state.

subjunctive – see **mood**.

suffix – short additions to the end of words to give them additional meanings and sometimes change the type of word, for example from adjective to adverb – **feliz**, *happy* → **felizmente**, *happily*.

superlatives – forms of adjectives and adverbs used to express the highest or lowest level – **o mais interessante**, *the most interesting*, **o mais depressa possível**, *as quickly as possible*.

syllable – a unit of pronunciation normally centred on a vowel sound which can be either a word in itself or a word segment – <u>o</u> (*the*, masculine), <u>a</u> (*the*, feminine), <u>o</u> nome (<u>no</u>-<u>me</u>), *name*, <u>a</u> mesa (<u>me</u>-<u>sa</u>), *table*.

tense – the different sets of verb changes used to express the time at which action or state is viewed as occurring (present, past, or future) – **eles moram lá**, *they live there*, **eles moraram lá há uns anos**, *they lived there some years ago*, **eles morarão lá daqui a uns anos**, *they will live there a few years from now*.

til – the Portuguese name for a wavy mark that is placed above a vowel to show a nasal sound, as in **não**, *no*.

um/uma – it can be a numeral (1), the indefinite article (2) or a pronoun (3) – (1) <u>um</u> bolo, por favor, não dois, *one cake, please, not two*; (2) **por favor, um bolo de amêndoa, não de chocolate,** *please, an almond cake, not chocolate*; (3) **por favor, um de amêndoa,** *please an almond one* (meaning *cake*).

. . . .

verb – a word to express an action, like **correr,** *to run,* or a state of being, like **ser,** *to be.*

. . . .

voiced – a consonant which is produced by the vibration of the vocal cords, like 'd' as opposed to 't', as in **dois,** *two.*

. . . .

vowel – a speech sound made by the vibration of the vocal cords, more open than a consonant and able to form a syllable, as in a, e, i, o, u – **porta fechada,** *closed door.*

. . . .

Index

Numbers refer to the chapter numbers of this book.

Lightning Source UK Ltd.
Milton Keynes UK
UKHW022022160123
415457UK00009B/152

9 781444 110678